MW00769445

A GUIDE TO PLAYING THE BAROQUE GUITAR

PUBLICATIONS OF THE EARLY MUSIC INSTITUTE
PAUL ELLIOTT, editor

A GUIDE TO PLAYING THE BAROQUE GUITAR

JAMES TYLER

INDIANA UNIVERSITY PRESS
BLOOMINGTON AND INDIANAPOLIS

This book is a publication of

Indiana University Press
601 North Morton Street
Bloomington, Indiana 47404-3797 USA

iupress.indiana.edu

Telephone orders   800-842-6796
Fax orders   812-855-7931
Orders by e-mail   iuporder@indiana.edu

© 2011 by James Tyler
All rights reserved

No part of this book may be reproduced or utilized in any form or
by any means, electronic or mechanical, including photocopying
and recording, or by any information storage and retrieval
system, without permission in writing from the publisher. The
Association of American University Presses' Resolution on
Permissions constitutes the only exception to this prohibition.

∞ The paper used in this publication meets the minimum requirements
of the American National Standard for Information Sciences—
Permanence of Paper for Printed Library Materials, ANSI Z39.48-1992.

Manufactured in the United States of America

Library of Congress Cataloging-in-Publication Data

Tyler, James.
A guide to playing the baroque guitar / James Tyler.
p. cm. — (Publications of the Early Music Institute)
Includes bibliographical references and index.
ISBN 978-0-253-22289-3 (pbk. : alk. paper) 1. Guitar—Performance—History. 2. Tablature (Music)—History—To 1800.
3. Guitar music—17th century—History and criticism. 4. Guitar music—18th century—History and criticism. 5. Guitar music—17th century. 6. Guitar music—18th century. I. Title.
ML1015.G9T956 2011
787.8709'032—dc22
2010033162

1 2 3 4 5   16 15 14 13 12 11

CONTENTS

CONTENTS

PART 2. AN ANTHOLOGY OF MUSIC FOR BAROQUE GUITAR 31
INTRODUCTION 32

PREFACE

THE AMOUNT OF GUITAR MUSIC produced during the late sixteenth through the middle of the eighteenth century is huge—second only to that of the lute. And like the latter, it ranges from the modest efforts of amateur musicians to the miniature masterpieces of the great court composers of Europe. Some of it even found its way to the New World. But while the lute's vast repertoire has become—thanks to recordings, publications, and lately, some new and improved music transcription software—both familiar and available throughout the world, the same cannot be said of the early guitar's, probably because of its rather unique notation.

Virtually all guitar music from the period was written in a tablature notation that looks somewhat similar to lute tablature. However, since the nature of the instrument, its idioms, and its playing techniques are significantly different from those of the lute (not to mention the classical guitar), so is its notation. For example, what might look like an arpeggio to a lutenist accustomed to reading lute tablature is simply a single-line, running scale passage in baroque guitar tablature. Guitar composers signaled arpeggios in other ways, and interpreting their tablatures requires an understanding of both the unique idioms and techniques of the instrument for which they composed and the ways in which they notated them.

The purpose of this book, then, is to provide a practical, point-by-point guide on how to read and interpret baroque guitar tablature, as well as suggestions for performing the music in an informed and stylish manner. Although it includes some quite rudimentary details and a few easier pieces along the way, it is intended not for beginners but for intermediate to advanced musicians—lutenists who wish to expand their performance horizons to include the baroque guitar; classical guitarists who wish to explore the repertoire on an actual five-course baroque-style instrument; and, of course, players of the baroque guitar, who might find some challenging additions to their present repertoire and some useful suggestions regarding interpretation.

Since there is no way to express in staff notation everything that is contained in the vast majority of baroque guitar tablatures, it is absolutely essential that players learn to read tablature. Therefore, part 1 deals with the main types of tablature and the meaning of the signs and symbols that one is most likely to encounter. It also includes a discussion of playing techniques.

Part 2—which is the heart of the book—is an anthology of representative guitar works, largely tested for effectiveness in public performance. Each work is prefaced by a commentary that gives a brief biography of the composer, a detailed explanation of the signs, symbols, and any idiosyncrasies unique to the piece or the particular publication in which it is found, as well as a description of the musical forms and other information that could provide clues to how the piece might have been performed. Each piece is presented in both tablature and staff notation. The latter, however, is for study and reference only and is not a transcription for classical guitar.

ACKNOWLEDGMENTS

THE PERFORMANCE OF PERIOD MUSIC involves a seamless blending of skill and scholarship. So said both of my esteemed teachers, Walter Kaye Bauer, with whom I studied the five-string classic banjo, tenor banjo, and mandolin as a teenager in Connecticut, and Joseph Iadone, with whom I later studied the lute.

Walter, a brilliant musician, music director, and composer, gave me a first-class grounding in technique and musicianship which served me well in all of my subsequent musical endeavors. As I would later discover, the techniques he taught me for playing the classic, gut-strung, finger-style (no nails) banjo of the late nineteenth through early twentieth century bore surprising similarities to those for the lute and baroque guitar. His insistence that I learn as much as possible about the composers and historical background of the music I was playing in order to interpret it in a manner that was true to the period would remain with me throughout my career as a performer and teacher.

Joseph Iadone was a musical prodigy and already a virtuoso on the double bass when, as Paul Hindemith's prize pupil at Yale University, he was instructed to take up the lute and play it in the maestro's famed Collegium Musicum. I suspect that most students of a modern instrument at a professional school of music would balk at having to learn to play an early instrument that isn't even from the same family, but not Joe. He embraced the lute and its music with passion and was soon a virtuoso on that instrument as well. Indeed, the major portion of his long career was as a lute soloist and member of the internationally renowned, pioneering early music ensemble, New York Pro Musica.

It was my good fortune to meet Joe in my late teens when he was teaching lute and early music performance at the Hartt College of Music in Hartford. Amazingly, he agreed to let me study with him privately and as a result profoundly changed my life. As a teacher, Joe didn't just give me lute lessons and help me develop a solo repertoire; he also gave me an appreciation of ensemble playing and some very important advice. First, do not automatically assume that what you read in reference books is correct; some of the information they contain is simply outdated, oft-repeated misinformation. And secondly, do not trust modern editions of early music until you've examined the originals (or facsimiles of the originals) yourself. I would later pass his advice on to my own students and it is implicit in my writings, including the present guide and anthology.

It would be impossible to acknowledge by name the countless librarians across the United States, Great Britain, and Europe, who were so helpful to me over the years when I invaded their libraries, usually arriving on short or with no notice on free days during concert tours. These patient, conscientious men and women enabled me to study and work with the original books and manuscripts that form the basis of this and previous publications, and I am most grateful to them all.

I would like to acknowledge a special colleague and friend, Dr. Nina Treadwell. Nina came from Australia to study with me when I was teaching at the University of Southern California. Even as a student she set standards in performance and scholarship that were hard to match; and now, a noted musicologist and revered teacher, she is passing on her ideas about historical performance practice to her own students at the University of California at Santa Cruz and giving her colleagues in the international community of researchers—myself included—a whole lot to think about.

At Indiana University Press, I thank Paul Elliott, editor of the Publications of the Early Music Institute; Music and Humanities editor Jane Behnken and her assistant, Sarah Wyatt Swanson; and Candace McNulty, copyeditor.

And finally, I would like to acknowledge the help of my patient and loving wife Joyce. For the past thirty-five years I have benefited from her uncompromising belief that one must always finish the things that one starts and that the ideas that are buzzing around chaotically in one's brain must be organized and communicated as clearly and succinctly as possible. She has worked in partnership with me in every way and in all my ventures, and there is no way that I can adequately thank her.

Pasadena, California
July 2010

PART 1.
THE BASICS

1

THE INSTRUMENT

IN THE LATE SIXTEENTH THROUGH the early eighteenth century the guitar was known as the Spanish guitar (Italian: *chitarra spagnola*). Throughout the period it had five courses (pairs) of gut strings. As a study of its music and the various contemporary references to its tuning and stringing reveal, the baroque instrument, unlike a lute or classical guitar, was not designed to have a true bass range. Its true range was tenor to low treble. (See the tuning/stringing charts in chapter 2.)

Structurally, the guitar's fingerboard was flush with the soundboard and its bridge a single bar of wood glued onto the soundboard like the bridge of a lute. Unlike the modern classical guitar, its frets were made of gut, not metal or ivory, and were tied around the neck rather than permanently inlaid. Movable frets were preferred to inlaid ones probably because they could be adjusted for fine-tuning. The number of frets varied from seven to ten on the neck, and museum instruments that have survived in their original state show that they never had more than two additional frets glued to their soundboards. One or two tablature sources call for notes up to the sixteenth fret, but these notes were probably played on the soundboard.

There was no standard string length; lengths varied from a long 74 cm to a short 58 cm, and body sizes varied accordingly. Guitars with a vaulted (or rounded) back were found just as frequently as the flat-backed models. Vaulted backs tended to be characteristic of Italian-made guitars and the Italian-style guitars built by German makers. The body shape, unlike that of a classical guitar, tended to be narrow with shallow sides.

2

TUNING AND STRINGING

IN THE BAROQUE PERIOD, pitch level, or nominal pitch, varied with the source of the guitar music. Some sources indicated a top first course that was called and read as d', but for most it was e'. The actual pitch, however, as measured by a modern tuning fork or electronic tuning device, could vary significantly depending on such factors as the size of the guitar and the other instruments one might be tuning it to.

Early guitarists tuned and strung their instruments in various ways, and not many of the music sources they played from specified which one to use. Apparently it was common practice to leave this to the player. Common practice for *them*, maybe, but how are modern players supposed to know which tuning and stringing arrangement to use for the baroque guitar music they want to play? The same way early players did: from the music itself, of course—but also from the few music sources that do provide some instructions. And according to those sources, there were three main ones.

The most common, which I call stringing A (see example 2.1), is **re-entrant,** i.e., without a bourdon on any of the courses. (The circled numbers in examples 2.1, 2.2, and 2.3 indicate the course numbers. The first course is usually, though not always, a single string.) A **re-entrant tuning** is one in which the courses are tuned to a pattern of rising, then falling intervals rather than to successively higher pitches from the bottom up. A **bourdon** is a thick string tuned an octave below the other string in the course. It sounds at the pitch level of a modern guitar's fourth (D) string and fifth (A) string. When a bourdon is used, it is the second string of the course (nearest to the first course) and not the first string, as one might find on a lute. In other words, when a course is played, it is the upper octave that is struck first by the thumb. This is important for technical and musical reasons, which will be explained in greater detail later.

The second most common tuning and stringing arrangement, which I call stringing B, is partially re-entrant and uses a bourdon on the fourth course *only* (example 2.2).

The third stringing arrangement uses bourdons on both the fourth and fifth courses. Although this stringing is closest to that of the classical guitar, it seems to have been the one least called for by composers of the more advanced baroque guitar music (stringing C, example 2.3).

EXAMPLE 2.1. Stringing A

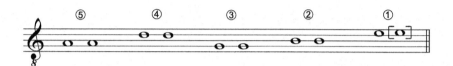

EXAMPLE 2.2. Stringing B

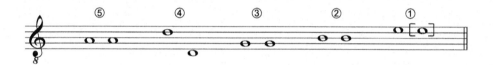

EXAMPLE 2.3. Stringing C

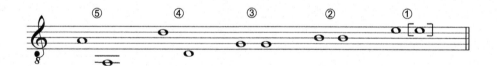

3

TECHNIQUE

Left-hand position and fingering for the baroque guitar are the same as for the lute and almost the same as for the classical guitar. Because the width of the baroque guitar's neck and its string spacing are much narrower than that of its modern counterpart, classical guitarists playing on a baroque-style instrument will find far fewer opportunities to keep their fingers parallel with the frets. Indeed, because baroque scale passages are not usually fingered in one position across the fingerboard but require much rapid shifting up and down the same string, they might find it more convenient to incline the fingers slightly toward the bridge, as a violinist or cellist would do. On the plus side, the baroque guitar's narrow neck facilitates rapid and complicated chord changes without tiring the left hand as much as it might on a wider-necked classical guitar.

Right-hand technique is essentially the same for the baroque guitar as for the lute. Most players held their right hand in a position with the thumb slightly extended toward the rosette and the little finger resting on the soundboard about two inches in front of the bridge, except when they played strummed chords. Typically, only the thumb and the index and second fingers were used, although the ring finger might also be called into service for certain types of chords.

Few technical instructions are provided in the music sources for baroque guitar, particularly in comparison to the voluminous amount found in modern guitar music and method books. But it seems as if the traditional, lute-like technique described above survived not only through the Baroque period, but also, as Fernando Sor's *Méthode pour la Guitarre* (Paris, 1830) attests, through the Classical. It is therefore recommended that Sor's excellent detailed instructions, which include several diagrams, be studied by all guitarists, even those specializing in the baroque instrument. Conveniently, there is a facsimile reprint of A. Merrick's English translation, which was first printed ca. 1832 and then ca. 1850. (See Selected Bibliography.) For our purposes, be certain to consult the facsimile reprint and not one of the modern editions, since the editors of the latter have taken it upon themselves to rewrite Sor's text and substitute modern classical guitar technique.

As many contemporary lute sources verify, most lutenists and guitarists of the Baroque period did not play with fingernails. This apparently held true during the Classical era as well. For example, on page 17 (of Merrick's translation), the highly influential Sor wrote: "Never in my life have I heard a guitarist whose playing was supportable, if he played with the nails. The nails can produce but very few gradations in the quality of the sound. . . ." Like the guitarists and lutenists of the past who did play with nails, modern guitarists wanting to play double-course instruments (particularly with gut strings) will have to make a few technical adjustments. For example, avoid positioning the right-hand knuckles parallel to the strings; instead hold the hand more obliquely, à la Sor. This adjustment will minimize the double-sounding note caused by nails. The thumbnail, if too long, can prove awkward; if it does, find a happy medium. Rest strokes are rarely called for in baroque guitar music; on a lightweight, lightly strung, double-course instrument built according to historical principles, use free strokes to achieve the best results.

4

READING TABLATURE NOTATION

FOR CENTURIES VIRTUALLY ALL GUITAR MUSIC was written in tablature, not staff notation, and there are several reasons for this. Tablature takes a more direct approach in presenting the music. It doesn't require the player to first interpret where the notes are on the fingerboard and what positions and fingerings to use; it *shows* you where the notes are and what positions and fingerings to use. The unique idioms called for in much of the best baroque guitar music cannot be presented with complete accuracy in staff notation—which is why many modern editors of baroque guitar music are obliged to present it with all of the features that distinguish it as baroque guitar music edited out, and why it is essential for any player truly interested in knowing how the music might originally have sounded to learn to read tablature.

ITALIAN TABLATURE

Italian and Spanish composers notated their guitar music in Italian number tablature and a special chord system known as *alfabeto*. In the Italian-style tablature illustrated in example 4.1 the five-line staff represents the five courses of the guitar. The top line represents the fifth course and the bottom line the first. Looking at a piece notated in Italian tablature is like looking at yourself and your guitar in a mirror that's sitting on your music stand; the strings appear in upside down order.

As shown in the example, the numbers on or between the lines represent the frets to be fingered: 0 = open string, 1 = first fret, 2 = second fret, 3 = third fret, etc. The tenth fret is sometimes represented by the Roman numeral x and the eleventh by ij. The example also includes an accurate representation of the tablature in staff notation as if transcribed for modern guitar.

Rhythm signs are usually presented as ordinary free-standing mensural notes above the staff. As shown in example 4.2, they are placed over specific numbers to indicate their time value. When a rhythm sign first appears, its time value remains valid until a new sign appears; the same sign is not usually repeated if the next note or chord is of the same duration. As shown in the second bar of the tablature (and its transcription into staff notation), the rhythm signs indicate only when the time value begins—not necessarily how long any individual voice should be held. The latter is left to the player.

EXAMPLE 4.1. Simple Italian tablature

EXAMPLE 4.2. Rhythm signs in Italian tablature

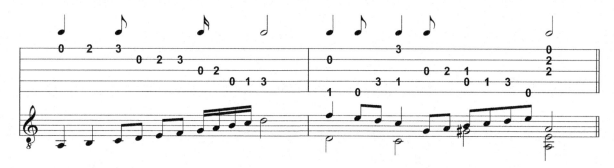

Example 4.3 is a short, simple piece from Carlo Calvi's book of 1646, which illustrates all of the tablature information given so far. Beneath the tablature is a transcription in modern guitar notation. It works well for this piece because Calvi's tablature book is one of the few sources that seems to call for stringing C (with bourdons on both the fourth and fifth courses).

EXAMPLE 4.3. Anonymous/Carlo Calvi (compiler), Canario,
Intavolatura di chitarra, e chitarriglia (Bologna, 1646), 27

9

ALFABETO

Beginning in the 1580s, a special tablature system was introduced that enabled composers to notate full chords without having to write out each individual note. Found either alone or mixed in with regular tablature, this notation was known as *alfabeto* for one exceedingly obvious reason—the chords are represented by specific letters of the alphabet. Unlike our modern chord system, however, the *alfabeto* letters do not correspond to a modern description of functional harmony. Rather, they're used purely as symbols, each letter signifying both a specific harmony and the position and inversion of that harmony on the fingerboard. For example, the *alfabeto* symbol **A** does not indicate an A major chord, but a G major chord in a particular position. This concept might seem a bit strange at first, but if the letters are simply memorized as the symbols they are, then reading *alfabeto* notation becomes quite easy and straightforward.

A few similar chord systems also emerged during this period, including the Spanish *cifras* system, which used numbers and a few other symbols instead of letters. However, the Italian *alfabeto* system was the one most commonly used, even by Spanish composers, as well as some German and French. As the occurrence of these other systems, relative to that of *alfabeto,* is rare and found mostly in simple accompaniments, I have not included any examples here.

Because of the guitar's tuning, stringing, and lack of basses (particularly in stringing A), when an *alfabeto* chord is strummed on a baroque guitar, the effect is that of a neutral, nearly inversionless sound unit. And indeed, baroque composers treated *alfabeto* chords essentially like root position block harmonies, regardless of their *actual* harmonic inversions. This is a defining characteristic of the baroque instrument; the same chords played on a classical guitar with its prominent basses would produce a strong aural presentation of the chords' inversions.

Example 4.4 is a chart of the letters A through M in the *alfabeto* chord system. It includes an accurate representation of the tablature in staff notation as if transcribed for classical guitar. Note that, historically, there is no letter J. Note also that only a few letter symbols actually need to be memorized at any one time. This will be explained fully in chapter 6 under the heading More about *Alfabeto.*

EXAMPLE 4.4. *Alfabeto* Chord System, A–M

Strums were notated in *alfabeto* tablature by means of short stroke lines that hang down from or stand up from the staff line. They are found immediately after the chord to be strummed. The direction of the signs indicates, of course, the direction in which the chords are to be strummed. Example 4.5 shows a simple chord progression notated in *alfabeto*. Only one staff line is required to show the down and up stroke signs. This is a common form of tablature when the music consists solely of *alfabeto* chords and nothing more complicated. Do not mistake the shorter lines which bisect the staff line for strokes; they are simply bar lines. In the transcription beneath the *alfabeto*, the direction of the chord stems corresponds to the down or up stroke signs in the tablature. The fundamentals of strumming technique are discussed at length in the next chapter.

EXAMPLE 4.5.

FRENCH TABLATURE

French composers presented their music in a tablature system that uses letters on the staff instead of numbers to represent the individual notes. This system was also used by English and some German composers. As illustrated in example 4.6, the top line of the five-line staff represents the first course and the bottom line represents the fifth—the reverse of Italian tablature; the letters sit above the relevant line or, occasionally, bisect the line. Note once again that, historically, there is no letter J.

EXAMPLE 4.6. Simple French tablature

As in Italian tablature, **rhythm signs** were usually presented as regular free-standing mensural notes above the staff, but occasionally flags without note heads were used. Be aware that these flags do not signify the same time values as regular notes. As the transcription beneath the tablature in example 4.7 shows, an upright stem without a flag

EXAMPLE 4.7. Rhythm signs in French tablature

equals a whole note; one flag = a half note; two flags = a quarter note; three flags = an eighth note, etc.

In French tablature, chords are generally written out in full or, as illustrated in example 4.8, only partially written out with the open courses omitted. Some French composers elected to use the Italian *alfabeto* system instead. Down and up strums or strokes are generally indicated by a stemmed note head *within* the staff. The direction of the stem indicates the direction of the strum. This sign also gives the time value of the strum. On beats where an internal stroke sign is given, a rhythm sign above the staff is unnecessary. Although the chords are presented with only the fingered notes indicated, it is assumed that the remaining open courses will also be included in the strum. (Strumming technique is discussed fully in the next chapter.)

Example 4.8 is a very brief excerpt from Lelio Colista's *Passacaille dite Mariona*. The piece is most likely for stringing B (with a bourdon on the fourth course only); however, a transcription for a guitar with bourdons on both the fourth and fifth courses is provided for players who are experiencing tablature for the first time. Modern violin bowing marks appear under certain chords in the transcription to indicate down and up strokes: the open square signifies a down stroke and the "v" an up stroke. Since a down stroke is naturally stronger than an up stroke, note that unexpected rhythmic accents are produced. These accents are intentional and the player should not be tempted to equalize the strokes. Just to make sure, modern accent marks have been included on the appropriate beats. Colista's *Passacaille dite Mariona* is presented in its entirety in part 2, where it is transcribed for stringing B.

EXAMPLE 4.8. Brief excerpt from *Passacaille dite Mariona* by Lelio Colista

5

THE FUNDAMENTALS OF *BATTUTO* (STRUMMING) TECHNIQUE

THERE IS NO REAL EQUIVALENT to *battuto* (Italian: *battente* or *battuto;* Spanish: *rasgueado*) for the modern classical guitar. Most players today equate the Spanish term for it, *rasgueado,* with flamenco guitar technique, but the two are very different, mainly because the high-tension stringing of the modern instrument demands a somewhat aggressive right-hand fingering style, while the much lower tension stringing of the baroque instrument encourages a more delicate approach.

Battuto technique involves both simple strokes and rhythmic ornamentation.

SIMPLE STROKES

Down strokes are played with the backs of the nails of the third, second, and first fingers and up strokes with at least the index finger. The strumming motion should come from the right-hand wrist alone and should not involve the forearm. The wrist should be bent outward (not level with the forearm), and the strokes should be executed using a twisting motion of the wrist. Some present-day guitarists play down strokes with just the flesh of the thumb for a gentler sound; however, this was not the original intention. A strum with the flesh of the thumb was indeed employed in the Baroque era, but it was considered a special effect and there was a specific sign in the notation to indicate when it was to be employed.

An extended passage of strummed chords should be played with the right hand over the fingerboard, not the soundboard. This position is specifically mentioned in some of the music sources, and guitarists are frequently depicted with their right hands thus in paintings and drawings of the period. The notes in a down strum should be played as close together as possible; although, if the passage is exceptionally long, some chords can be spread for the sake of variety. Unless otherwise indicated in the music, on a down stroke all five courses should be struck. On an up stroke, however, using the index finger alone, it's only necessary to strike three or four.

The chords can be strummed loudly and vigorously, very softly, or anything in between, depending, of course, on the musical context. Full control of the right-hand wrist is essential to achieve these nuances of sound. Strummed chords are an integral part of baroque guitar technique and must be practiced diligently so that, when interspersed with lute-style passages, they sound neither tentative nor obtrusive.

RHYTHMIC ORNAMENTATION

The simple strumming technique described above should be augmented with rhythmic ornamentation; however, when precisely to do so seems to have been left up to the player. The two main forms of rhythmic ornamentation are (in Italian) the **trillo** and the **repicco**. The *trillo,* described in different ways by seventeenth-century guitarists, is basically a series of rapid down and up strokes played either with the index finger of the right hand or with various combinations of the index and thumb. It is used to augment the sound or fill in the texture of chord passages. The guitarist Foscarini advocates playing two strokes for each printed one, and he leaves it to the player to decide when to use it. Other guitarists suggest three or four strokes for each printed one. Example 5.1 illustrates how the player might add *trilli* to the harmonic pattern known as the *Bergamasca.*

The *repicco* is similar to the *trillo,* but is often more intricate and rhythmically charged. It involves four strokes: a controlled use of the full down stroke, followed by a down and an up stroke using just the thumb, and ending with an up stroke using just the index finger. Occasionally, *repicci* are found in the music fully written out. For the transcription in example 5.2, I've used modern designations for the right-hand fingers (p = thumb and i = index finger). The player should articulate the four strokes of the *repicco* with care, so that each is heard uniformly and distinctly. Practice them slowly at first and then bring them up to the speed of approximately quarter note = 160 while still retaining a relaxed and fluent right-hand wrist movement. Don't forget to hold your hand over the fingerboard, not the soundboard. After mastery of the basic pattern, nearly any chord shown as a single stroke in the music can be played in the rhythmic pattern shown in example 5.2, or in other patterns, such as the two illustrated in example 5.3.

EXAMPLE 5.1

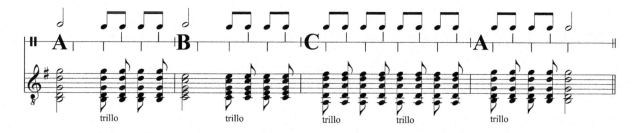

EXAMPLE 5.2

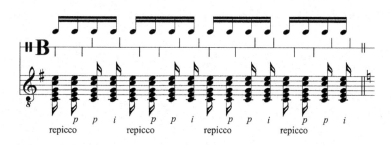

EXAMPLE 5.3

6

READING MIXED TABLATURE NOTATION

AFTER THE 1630S, Italian guitar composers began using a mixture of simple Italian number tablature and one-line *alfabeto*. Inserting the *alfabeto* letter symbols and stroke signs within the normal five-line system not only enabled them to notate melodic lines efficiently, but also eliminated the need to write out common chords in full. In most mixed tablatures, chords are only written out if they are in some way unusual.

The new mixed tablature also enabled composers to notate, with a full range of signs and symbols, how they intended their music to be performed.

PERFORMANCE MARKINGS

Dots are sometimes found on staff lines in conjunction with a strummed chord. These dots tell us that a **selective chord voicing** for the performance of *alfabeto* or other strummed chords is intended, and that the marked course(s) should not be included in the stroke. In some instances these courses are not marked and the decision is left to the ears and the common sense of the player. Sometimes selective chord voicing can present technical challenges, but that—together with the execution of some of the more complicated stroke patterns described above—only goes to show how sophisticated a technique baroque guitar strumming can be.

Example 6.1 illustrates the use of dots for selective chord voicing. In the first instance, the *alfabeto* **B** is played without striking the first course, and in the second instance, likewise the *alfabeto* **I**.

Another performance marking, illustrated in example 6.2, is the diagonal line that signifies **tenuto**—the holding of certain notes in the bass or treble voices of a passage.

Sometimes performance marks for **right-hand fingering** are found under certain notes. These marks include . = index finger, .. = middle finger, etc. (See example 6.3.) In some French sources a short, hanging line under a note indicates that the note should be played with the thumb.

For **left-hand fingering**, either the numbers one through four are used, or one, two, three, or four dots are placed beside the notes; obviously, the latter works better for music that uses the Italian and Spanish number tablatures. (See example 6.3.)

EXAMPLE 6.1

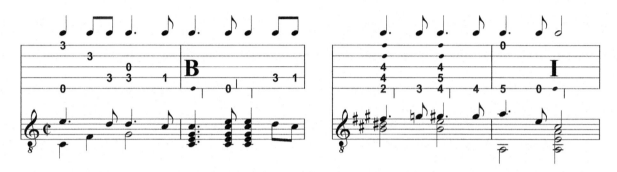

EXAMPLE 6.2

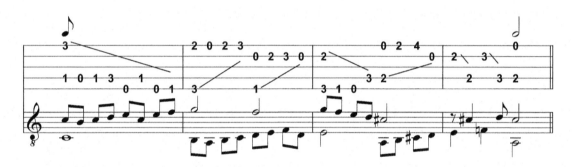

EXAMPLE 6.3

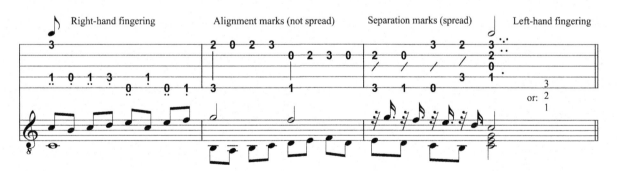

A **vertical mark** aligning two or more notes in a chord means that the notes are intended to be played simultaneously, not spread or arpeggiated. Conversely, a **diagonal mark** found between the notes in a chord signals that the notes should be spread. (See example 6.3.)

ORNAMENT SIGNS

Ornaments are embellishments to certain individual notes in a passage. They were generally called "graces" in England, *abilimenti* or *tremoli* in Italy, *agréements* in France, and *habilidades* or *afectos* in Spain. A whole range of ornament signs is found in mixed tablatures. Unfortunately, a sign used by one composer to mean one type of ornament was often used by other composers to mean another type. In some cases the appearance of an ornament sign doesn't even signify a specific ornament but merely that an appropriate ornament should be played at that point in the music! For those reasons, the systemizing of signs that one finds in many modern reference works seems both misleading and pointless. Unless a composer provided specific instructions regarding the ornament signs he used in his book (a rare occurrence), it is up to the player to decide which ornament he intended when he used a particular sign.

Some ornament signs are less ambiguous than others. For example, most composers used a sharp sign to indicate **vibrato,** which was regarded as a single ornament on a selected note in the Baroque period; it was not used continuously as it is in modern bowed string playing, or as a component of playing technique, as it is for the classical guitar. As the guitarist Foscarini described it ca. 1630, vibrato was performed by removing the thumb from the neck of the instrument to achieve the best result, and jiggling the finger that is stopping the note most vigorously.

The **slur** was considered an ornament also. It was notated in the same manner as it is today, with a curved line above or below two or more notes in a passage. Sometimes a long slur sign that resembles a modern phrase mark is found over several notes that cross over from one course to another. When this sign appears, it is assumed that the composer is leaving it to the player to divide the one long slur—logically—into smaller ones for each course.

Slurs were often used to produce some rather striking rhythmic effects. As the first note of a slur is the only one that is plucked, it is naturally stronger than the others, which can result in some ear-catching rhythmic stresses throughout the passage. To illustrate, example 6.4 is an excerpt from Francesco Corbetta's *Chiacona* (1648) with my added accent marks in the transcription. This piece is presented in its entirety in part 2.

The **arpeggio,** like vibrato, was regarded as an ornament in the Baroque period. Its sign, ⁄ or ꞉⁄꞉ found under a chord (be it in *alfabeto* notation or fully written out) and below the staff, indicates that the chord should be broken up into individual notes, sometimes in a quite elaborate manner. Unlike the regular arpeggiation patterns in classical or romantic music, the patterns for baroque arpeggios, as shown in example 6.5, tended to be made up of uneven and irregular numbers of individual notes—perhaps seven, ten, or fifteen—in a rising and falling pattern for each beat unit in the bar. Of course, arpeg-

EXAMPLE 6.4

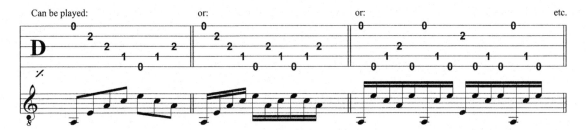

gios could also be executed in even note numbers in a simple rising and falling pattern, but one rarely finds anything even remotely resembling the "Alberti basses" of the Classical era, or in the style of a modern folk guitar accompaniment. Given the improvisatory nature of arpeggios, particularly the ones with uneven patterns, the time value of the written note can be lengthened if the player so desires.

EXAMPLE 6.5

Trill signs are frequently encountered in the tablatures, but composers rarely explained how to perform them, nor is there any consistency or consensus among them as to the sign. Italian composers commonly placed an upper or lower case letter t beside a note to indicate that a trill—which they called *tremolo*—should be played. Some Italian writers also called it a *trillo,* not to be confused with the strummed rhythmic ornament of the same name, while Spanish writers called it the *trino* or *aleado.*

Other tremolo signs found in the tablatures include a simple dot beside the note, a small x, or a dot-slash-dot. Some composers even used the same sign to indicate a different ornament in one of their own subsequent publications! As previously advised, one should always check the preface of the guitar book one is playing from to see if the composer has provided any specific instructions.

The baroque tremolo was not played like any type of modern tremolo. Regardless of the sign used, Italian composers expected a **main note trill** to be played as follows: Pluck the written note and hammer on with the left hand to the note above, then pull off from there back to the main note. For a simple trill, the above motion normally is done only once and produces a sounding of three quick distinct notes as one unit. If the trill sign occurs at a final cadence, however, or at another point of more than passing duration, then several repetitions of the hammering on and pulling off motions are expected.

While the main note trill is characteristic of Italian and Spanish music, French composers tended to use an **upper note trill** (*tremblement*) played as follows: Pluck the note *above* the written one; then, with the left hand, pull off to the main (written) note, hammer on to the upper note again, and then pull off to the main note. This motion involves sounding *four* quick distinct notes as one unit. Like the main note trill, it can be lengthened at cadences. In order to produce a stylish interpretation of the music at hand, it is important to heed the differences in performance practice between the two main musical cultures of the time—the Italian and the French.

The **mordent** was another commonly used ornament. The Italians and Spanish called it a *mordente,* and the French a *martellement* or *pincé.* Needless to say, signs for it varied from one composer to another and include: a modern-looking double sharp sign; a small, horizontal, curved line below the note; a vertical line following the note; a small v; and a small cross. The baroque mordent is similar to a modern lower mordent. It is played by plucking the main note, then, with the left hand, quickly pulling off to a lower note, and then back again to the main note. This motion involves sounding three quick distinct notes as one unit.

And finally, there's the **appoggiatura,** called an *esmorsata, apoyamento,* or *ligadura* in Spanish sources, and a *cheute* in French. There are two types: the **descending appoggiatura,** which is played on the beat starting on a note above the main (written) note, and then quickly pulling off it to the main one; and the **ascending appoggiatura,** which is played by starting on a note *below* the main one, then hammering on to the main one. The ascending appoggiatura should, perhaps, be played in a more languid manner than the descending, particularly at a cadence. The sign for the descending appoggiatura is often a small, horizontal, curved line above or below the main note, though some composers used a small **x** and others a small **t**. The sign for the ascending appoggiatura is a small curved line.

While there are several modern reference works that deal with ornamentation, most center on the plentiful information found in keyboard sources. As keyboard practice and technique often produce slightly different results, it is arguably best to focus on information that relates specifically to plucked instruments. Although the information presented above is only a rough guide, all of it is verified by the sparse details found in original guitar and lute sources. Since composers applied these signs in such an unsystematic manner, an interpretation of the ones that appear in each of the pieces selected for the anthology in part 2 can be found in the commentaries that precede them.

MORE ABOUT *ALFABETO*

Another reason *alfabeto* was considered such a logical and efficient notation system is its use of **movable chord shapes.** Many composers put position numbers over the letter symbols that represent certain chord shapes (harmonies). These numbers tell us that a chord shape different from the one normally understood by the letter symbol is wanted. Since these "new" chord shapes are also represented by letter symbols that come later in the alphabet, the numbers over the letters make memorizing the later ones unnecessary. (For example, in the full *alfabeto* system G3 = Y, H3 = Z, etc.) As the staff notation in example 6.6 clearly shows, a number over a letter in the tablature designates the fret at which the lowest finger in the chord shape should be placed.

EXAMPLE 6.6

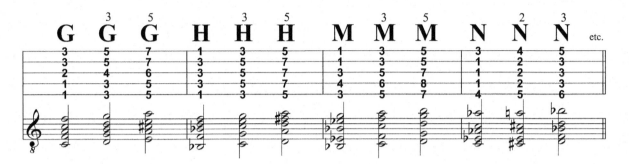

Since not all composers used movable chord shape numbers, a reference chart illustrating the complete, universal *alfabeto* system was made. This system was used for over two centuries, and the chart appears not only in Italian sources of guitar music, but also in many French, Spanish, German, and English ones. Considering that there are at least four hundred printed and manuscript collections comprising thousands of solos and song accompaniments with *alfabeto* notation, baroque guitar players really need to become familiar with it.

EXAMPLE 6.7. Universal *Alfabeto* Reference Chart

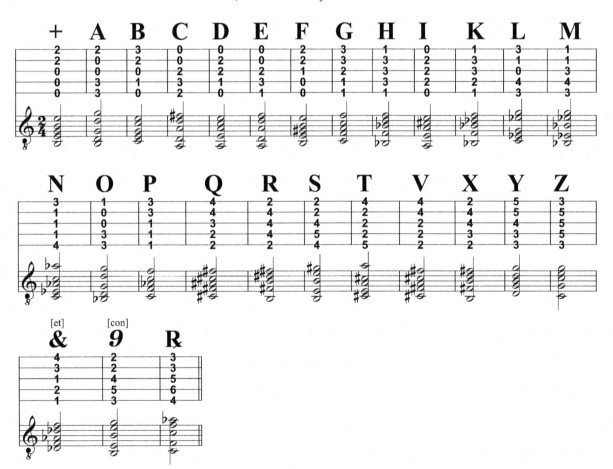

Several composers expanded the system by adding signs to the *alfabeto* letters to indicate chords with dissonances or suspensions, which they explained in their prefaces. These additions are rarely encountered, are unique to each composer, and need not be memorized. Example 6.8 is a chart of dissonant chords from Foscarini's ca. 1632 collection, and example 6.9 is from Calvi's 1646 anthology. Notice that on Foscarini's chart only the fingered notes of the chord are notated. It is assumed that the remaining courses are open and will be sounded in the chord.

EXAMPLE 6.8. Giovanni Paolo Foscarini, *"alfabeto dissonante"*

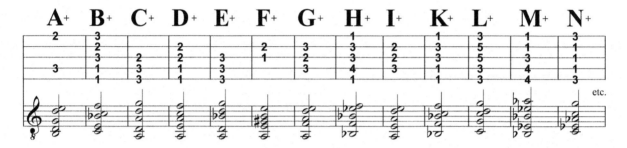

EXAMPLE 6.9. Carlo Calvi, *"alfabeto falso"*

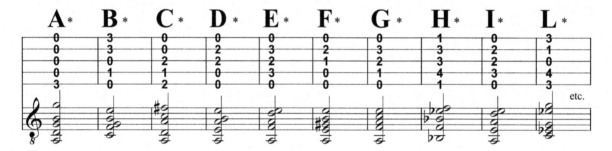

7

IDIOMS UNIQUE TO THE BAROQUE GUITAR

"INVERSIONLESS" CHORDS

When chords are sounded on a guitar that is strung without basses, no strongly audible inversions are produced; the chords are heard as units of pure block harmony. Since the clarity and transparency of the chords allowed the words of solo songs to be easily heard and understood, this feature made the baroque guitar an ideal instrument for the accompaniment of "the new music" (Italian monody), and many of the early monody composers included *alfabeto* tablature, with or without a bass line for another instrument, in their collections. Example 7.1 presents the chart of *alfabeto* chords with a transcription beneath showing the actual voicing of each chord when played on a guitar strung without basses (stringing A). "Inversionless" chord voicing cannot be achieved on any other plucked instrument of the period, nor, of course, on the bass-rich modern guitar. Indeed, combined with the techniques for strumming the chords described in chapter 4, this idiom was one of the chief defining features of the baroque instrument.

EXAMPLE 7.1

CAMPANELAS

The use of harp- or bell-like effects in scale passages is another important guitar idiom. There is no widespread term for this effect, which the Italians called *campanelle,* but the Spanish guitarist Gaspar Sanz, who espoused Italian technique, called it *campanelas* (little bells). It is performed by plucking each note of a scale (or other melodic passage) on a different course and employing as many open strings as possible, thus allowing each scale note to ring on longer than would otherwise be possible. The effect is similar to playing a rapid scale on the open strings of a harp without damping any of them; successive notes ring on and blend into the previous ones. Example 7.2 shows how this idiom looks on the page for a guitar using stringing A; it, too, cannot be achieved on a modern guitar. The long phrase marks in the transcription beneath the tablature are used to indicate that each of the separate notes under the mark blends into its neighbor.

EXAMPLE 7.2

THE SELECTIVE PLAYING OF BOURDONS

Regardless of which of the three main stringing arrangements one uses, there will always be a few anomalies in the scale patterns. This occurs because there are only five courses available to the composer, and when the effect he wishes to achieve requires more than five, the result is the appearance of an octave leap. A technique that can eliminate most of these anomalies involves the selective playing of one or both strings in an octave-strung course. In order for this technique to work, the upper octave string of, say, the fourth course must be placed in the *outer* position—nearest the fifth course—and the lower octave string (the bourdon) nearest the first course. This placement of the upper octave is commonly found on many traditional types of guitar, including the *jarana jarocha* of Mexico, the *tiple* of Colombia, and the *charango* of Bolivia and other Latin American countries, as well as on the twelve-string guitar. The great violin and guitar maker Antonio Stradivari specifies this arrangement on one of his ca. 1700 design patterns. It is also described by guitarists Michel Corrette in 1763 and Paixão Ribeiro in 1789, and shown in a number of contemporary pictures.

A course strung in this manner enables the guitarist to play either the upper and lower strings together or the upper string alone, depending upon the musical requirements of the scale passage, thus eliminating most octave-leap anomalies. The exercises in example 7.3 demonstrate this concept. They are for a guitar using stringing B (with a bourdon on the fourth course). An asterisk has been placed under the notes in the tablature where the music seems to indicate that the upper octave string and the bourdon should be played together. Otherwise, only the upper octave string should be sounded.

Tuning charts found in two anonymous sources suggest that, occasionally, the third course was strung with an upper octave (g') instead of unisons. Certain passages in the music of a number of composers, including Gaspar Sanz (1674) and Ludovico Roncalli (1692), imply the same. In order to string a guitar in this fashion, one would have needed either a smallish instrument with a relatively short vibrating string length, or one tuned lower in pitch than today's standard of A = 440. Otherwise, the tension of the upper octave on the third course would have been too great for a gut string, which has a lower breaking point than a modern (nylon) string of the same thickness. The information given for the selective playing of fourth- and fifth-course bourdons also applies to the octave stringing of the third course.

EXAMPLE 7.3. Selective playing of bourdons

Excerpt from: Prelude by A. M. Bartolotti, ca. 1655

etc.

8

A NOTE ON *BASSO CONTINUO*

AS PREVIOUSLY NOTED, the baroque guitar, like the harpsichord, organ, lute, theorbo, harp, lirone, and other chord-playing instruments, was also used to accompany the voice, solo instruments, and vocal and instrumental ensembles. This involved reading from a bass clef line with or without the figures beneath the notes that helped the accompanist to realize the intended harmonies (*basso continuo*). The harmonies were never written out in full in the Baroque era (as they were for accompanists in the Classical and Romantic periods), but were improvised from the bass line. Because of the improvisatory nature of the accompaniments, not to mention some basic differences between the various instruments playing them, the results, too, could be quite different—even if the continuo players were all reading from the same bass line. The accompanists rarely wrote down their improvised parts, because it was assumed that the same piece performed with a different soloist and under different circumstances would likely result in a different accompaniment. Continuo players needed to be flexible in the event that the soloist decided to perform the piece at a different tempo or use more or less rubato, more, less, or different *passagi* (extended improvised scale passages), etc. And the figured bass system allowed them this flexibility.

Even though the baroque guitar has few actual bass notes, guitarists were expected to read from the figured bass line. They also used the *alfabeto* chord system to supplement or replace the figures; so did players of other plucked instruments such as the mandolino, cittern, and harp. A great many song collections of the period include a chart in which bass notes are correlated to *alfabeto* chord symbols, and the *alfabeto* chord symbols are used in lieu of a figured bass line to accompany the songs.

Many books of guitar solos also contain at least some information on reading and playing from a figured bass line, and some books were specifically devoted to the topic as it relates to the guitar—Nicola Matteis's *The False Consonances of Musick, or Instructions for the Playing a True Base upon the Guitarre . . .* (London, 1682) and Santiago de Murcia's *Resumen de Acompañar la Parte con la Guitarra* ([Antwerp], 1714) being prime examples.

Continuo accompaniment was an important component of guitar playing during the Baroque period, and it should be today as well. Unfortunately, due to the strong bias that most musicologists have toward keyboard instruments , nearly all modern academic books on continuo playing contain only the fussy, textbook-like "rules" of maintaining voice-leading, chord voicing, and prescribed textures that pertain to keyboards, and which relate little if at all to the information found in the original sources that deal with *plucked* instruments. It is therefore important to seek out the few modern writings that deal specifically with the fundamentals of the figured bass system as it relates to our instruments. A good overview of the topic is Jack Ashworth and Paul O'Dette's chapter "Basso Continuo" in *A Performer's Guide to Seventeenth-Century Music*. Also useful is Monica Hall's article "The Five-Course Guitar as a Continuo Instrument" in *Lute News*. The only modern book containing actual instructions for playing continuo on plucked instruments is Nigel North's *Continuo Playing on the Lute, Archlute and Theorbo*. In part two of the book, North includes an excellent explanation of the basics, which can also be applied to the guitar. For further details regarding these publications, see the Selected Bibliography.

Part 1 of the present book concludes with example 8.1, a short, simple dance piece that illustrates how a guitar might have been employed as the continuo-playing member of an ensemble. It involves the easiest of continuo accompaniments. The *alfabeto* tablature, which appears to be a "chord chart" for a popular piece dating from as early as 1551 and known elsewhere as Almande Prince, Pavan of Albart, and *Si je m'en vois*, is from Giovanni Antonio Colonna's book of 1620, while the tune and the bass line with figures are from various contemporary ensemble versions. The tempo should be a moderate two half note beats in a bar at about MM 54. The guitar part can and should be varied as per the instructions given in chapter 5 under the heading Rhythmic Ornamentation.

EXAMPLE 8.1. *Balletto* (Almande Prince), Giovanni Ambrosio Colonna,
Intavolatura di chitarra alla spagnuola (Milan, 1620), 56

PART 2.
AN ANTHOLOGY OF MUSIC FOR BAROQUE GUITAR

INTRODUCTION

Although an abundance of facsimile editions of baroque guitar music is available today, many of the original prints and manuscripts were presented in a manner that could be off-putting to players not used to dealing with them. Editors and players accustomed to reading from these original sources or from editions that use re-creations of authentic typefaces, partial rhythm signs, and bars split over two systems will doubtless frown upon the tablature style I've adopted in this anthology. However, my aim is to produce editions that are not only accurate but also clear, readable, and easily accessible to all players, including those who are new to baroque guitar tablature.

I have included all of the original tablature notation, *alfabeto* symbols, performance markings, and ornament signs in my editions, but I have used modern typefaces. Apart from correcting mistakes and misprints, the only alteration I've made to the original tablatures is in the presentation of rhythm signs. The composers or copyists of the selected pieces rarely repeat rhythm signs in passages comprising notes of the same duration. As this can result in a whole succession of bars without a rhythm sign, I have reiterated the signs and, for the sake of rhythmic precision, beamed them in rhythmic units throughout, even if they were not presented that way in the originals.

The commentary that precedes each of the pieces or suites includes a record of misprints or mistakes found in the originals as well as any editorial signs or additions. The pieces are presented first in tablature. This version is intended for reading, performance, and historical reference, as it contains all of the original performance indications, spellings, and so on. A transcription in staff notation (one-line treble clef sounding an octave lower) follows. This is not a guitar transcription. As noted in part 1, except for the pieces that are suitable for a guitar using stringing C, the staff notation transcriptions in the anthology cannot be played on a classical guitar without seriously distorting the music. The staff notation transcriptions are given for reference and study purposes only as they show pitches, voice leading, and other details in the tablature that some might find useful.

9

PIECES SUITABLE FOR STRINGING A

PAVANAS POR LA D—GASPAR SANZ (1675)

Gaspar Sanz (b. Aragon, mid 17th C–d. early 18th C) was a clergyman who received a bachelor of theology degree and *licenciado en filosofia* at the University of Salamanca. It was probably his priestly duties that took him first to Naples and then to Rome, where he studied composition and guitar with such notable musicians as Pietro Andrea Ziani and Lelio Colista, among others. Upon returning to Spain, Sanz published his influential two-volume treatise *Instruccion de Musica sobre la Guitarra Española* in 1674–75. (A later edition appeared in 1697.) The work was dedicated to his pupil, the Spanish prince Don Juan of Austria, brother of King Carlos II. Other guitarists appropriated portions of it for their own publications until well into the eighteenth century.

Pavanas por la D is found in volume two (1675). Although it has no *alfabeto* chord symbols, the "*por la D*" (for the D) in its title refers to the *alfabeto* symbol for the key of A minor. The piece is based on a well-known Italian ground (harmonic pattern) called the *Pavaniglia*, which appears in countless versions from around 1546 to the middle of the eighteenth century. In 1578, the Spanish composer Cabezón used it as a dance piece, which he called the *Pavana italiana*. English writers usually called it the Spanish pavan, and the Spanish called it the *pavanas*. Sanz uses the harmonic pattern in its customary sixteen-bar form for a statement and two variations.

Three ornament signs are found in the piece: a small **t** to indicate a main note trill (Spanish: *trino*); a curved line above a note (⌒), as in bar 5, to indicate an ascending appoggiatura (Spanish: *apoyamento*); and a sharp or pound sign to denote a strong, fast vibrato (Spanish: *temblor*). The series of dots below notes or chords found in several bars are Sanz's original left-hand fingerings. The pairs of parallel lines found in bars 16 and 32 simply indicate the end of one section and the beginning of the next.

In his preface, Sanz describes various stringing arrangements used by different guitarists and specifically recommends the fully re-entrant one as the most suitable for refined music. As implied in bars 22, 35, 39, and 40, he may also call for an octave-strung third course. In those bars I have added a + sign under the staff as a means of bringing the open third course g's in question to the player's attention. Where I have so marked, players who aren't using an upper octave on the third course can play an upper octave g on the first or second course.

I suggest playing the piece at a tempo of about half note = 60, making certain to maintain a steady two beats per bar. In the seventeenth century rhythms and tempos were still derived from the traditional *Tactus* system, which was based on a down and up motion of the hand in two—regardless of the meter. This feeling of two in a bar makes a world of difference to the phrasing, so please resist the temptation to feel it in the modern sense of four quarter note beats.

Sanz set the first two statements of the *Pavanas* entirely in lute style (Spanish: *punteado*) with no strummed chords. Since pavans are stately dances, go for a somewhat grand, dignified mood, even though this particular pavan is set at a slightly brisker pace than other examples. Pay special attention to the spicy discords in bars 3 and 11. Although these are only two- or three-note chords, they still should be spread to emphasize the discords. In the second statement of the ground, note the slight variations in harmony beginning in bar 17 and the introduction of unexpected dominant sevenths in bars 18 and 19.

The third statement of the ground at bar 33 is written entirely in cascading *campanelas,* which pour out in a nonstop stream of single-line notes. This section is usually omitted from the transcriptions of the piece for classical guitar. Played with the proper technique on a baroque guitar, Sanz's *campanelas* can sound quite colorful and impressive, so a repeat of the section is highly recommended.

A facsimile of Sanz's *Pavanas* can be found in Frank Koonce, *The Baroque Guitar in Spain and the New World,* and a facsimile of the 1697 edition of Sanz's *Instruccion de Musica sobre la Guitarra Espanola,* published by Minkoff (Geneva, 2004), is available from OMI (see Selected Bibliography).

Editorial

An apparent misprint in bar 39 has been corrected: the first two eighth notes were pitched at g and b instead of b and g.

Pavanas por la D

Gaspar Sanz

Instruccion de Musica sobre la Guitarra Española (Zaragoza, 1675), Book II, plate 10

Gaspar Sanz, *Pavanas por la D*

SUITE OF ENGLISH TUNES—ELIZABETH CROMWELL'S MANUSCRIPT (CA. 1684)

The five pieces selected and presented here as a continuous suite are all anonymous settings of popular tunes found in a manuscript now in the Houghton Library at Harvard University. The manuscript was personally compiled by "The Right Honorable Lady Elizabeth Cromwell," as she is identified in a fine engraving after a portrait by Sir Godfrey Kneller. Elizabeth (1674–1709) was the daughter of Vere Essex Cromwell, the seventh Baron Cromwell. She was a contemporary of Samuel Pepys, the well-known diarist and secretary of the navy, who, like Elizabeth, also played the guitar. Her manuscript contains thirty-five Restoration-era dances and popular pieces of which the present five are typical. The brief tuning chart on folio 3 implies the use of stringing A, and this is borne out by the idiomatic requirements of the pieces. The music is quite simple and mostly involves single-line melodies with few chords.

The first piece in the suite, "The Shepherds Dance," is probably related to an entire range of ballad tunes, which often are found under the title "The Shepherd's Delight."

There are hundreds of tunes in the Morris dance repertoire, but the origin of the second piece in the suite, "The Morice [Morris] Dance," thus far has not been discovered.

The origin of the third piece, however, is known. "The Cannaris [Canary, Canaries]" is based on the popular French song *Marion pleure*, of which there are many contemporary settings for lute, mandore, lyra viol, keyboard, and guitar. One of the guitar settings, found in Paris (F Psg MS 2351, fol. 22v) is nearly identical in places to the Cromwell version, and it was definitely intended for stringing A. The tune in the Cromwell version is not related to any of the other dance pieces titled "Canario" by Italian or Spanish writers (including Gaspar Sanz).

The origin of the fourth piece, "I Know Not What/a Gigge [Jig]," has not yet been discovered.

And finally, "Black Jack" was known as a country dance, which, with the addition of a text and under the title "Black Joke," became an exceptionally bawdy street song. The earliest known version of the tune is found in John Playford's *The Dancing Master* (7th edition, 1665). The tune itself remained popular in the United States until well into the nineteenth century.

I suggest the following tempos for each of the pieces: nos. 1 and 2 should have a pulse or beat of two half notes in a bar at MM = 80; no. 3 should maintain a brisk quarter note = 152; no. 4, two beats per bar of quarter note = 120; and no. 5, quarter note = 144.

There are two ornament signs present: the # sign, which probably indicates a main note trill on the first course; and a comma sign, which indicates that a quick descending appoggiatura should be played. (See part 1, chapter 6—Performance Markings.) Few right-hand fingerings are given in the manuscript.

As these are short dance pieces, it is appropriate practice to repeat sections within each piece and to play the pieces with a *da capo*.

To date, there is no facsimile edition available of Elizabeth Cromwell's manuscript.

Suite of English Tunes

Anonymous

Elizabeth Cromwell Guitar Book
Harvard University, Houghton Library, Ms. Mus. 139, fols. 4–8ᵛ (1684–85)

I know not what / a Gigge

Black Jack

Editorial

I have added the dots on the staff at bars 11 and 12 of piece no. 4, "I Know Not What / a Gigge," as a reminder to use selective chord voicing. I have also added the time signatures and a missing bar in piece no. 5.

Suite of English Tunes

CORRENTE NONA—FERDINANDO VALDAMBRINI (1646)

The Roman guitarist Ferdinando Valdambrini published two books, the first in 1646 and the second in 1647. There is a faint possibility that he may have been the Roman painter Ferdinando Valdambrini (1623–ca. 1690). His two books contain many high-quality pieces, including toccatas, *corrente, balletti,* songs, and other dance pieces. The second of the two contains an important explanation of continuo practice for guitar.

A *corrente* is an Italian courtship dance with a brisk tempo and hop-step combinations for its choreography. I suggest a tempo of quarter note = 138. The dance is related to the French *courante* and the English coranto and is often found as part of a suite, which is probably how Valdambrini intended it, as he presented his dance music in groups under the name of each dance. This is the ninth (*nona*) in his series of *corrente.* Interestingly, players of the period created their own suites, which could consist of the music of one or more composers.

In his introduction, Valdambrini unequivocally calls for stringing A. He also says that he places two dots under a note to indicate that an ornament should played, the nature of which he leaves to the taste of the player. I suggest playing them as main note trills. Take care not to mistake these dots for right-hand fingering marks! The term *partita* in the music means a variation of the previous material.

Unfortunately, there are no facsimile editions of Valdambrini's books available at this writing.

Editorial

I have inserted dots on some of the staves to indicate selective chord voicing for certain strummed chords, and I have interpreted the rhythm sign of a single flag and the number 3 found in bars 22, 26, 42, and 46 to mean triplets.

41

Corrente nona

Ferdinando Valdambrini

Libro primo d'intavolatura di chitarra (Rome, 1646), 14

42

Corrente nona

Ferdinando Valdambrini, *Corrente nona*

44

ALLEMANDE-SARABANDE—ANTOINE CARRÉ (1671)

According to the title pages of his two books of guitar music, which were published in Paris in 1671 and ca. 1675 respectively, Antoine Carré was a French nobleman—"le Sieur de la Grange." The *Allemande* and *Sarabande* are from the first of the two, *Livre de Guitarre contenant plusieurs pieces,* which he dedicated to Sophia, the Princesse Palatine. Sophia (1630–1714) was the daughter of the Elector Palatine Frederick V and the English princess Elizabeth Stuart, who were in exile in the Hague, where they were known as the Winter King and Queen of Bohemia. Sophia was also the mother of the future Hanoverian king of England George I. The book bore the coveted "Privilège du Roy" imprint (the "Roy" being Louis XIV), granted on 18 February 1671. His second book was also dedicated to a member of the aristocracy in the Hague—Mary, Princess of Orange, whose son, William III of the Netherlands, was crowned King of England in 1689.

Carré's 1671 book contains various items organized by key but not put into suites, and a treatise on playing *basso continuo*. For his solos he provides a guitar tuning chart, which shows unequivocally that they were to be played on a guitar using stringing A, and—curiously—that the relative pitch of its first course was at d'; that is, a guitar tuned a whole tone lower than the customary e'. In his instructions for playing *basso continuo*, however, it is clear that he had a higher pitched e'-tuned guitar in mind, and that, for continuo playing, he recommended using a bourdon on the fourth course. His solos work well with either stringing.

Originally the *allemande* was a rather vigorous dance in Germany, England, and Italy; however, in the France of Carré's time—the age of Lully—it was slowed down and became the introductory piece in a suite. As one contemporary writer described the French version as serious and dignified, I would suggest playing Carré's *Allemande* at a tempo of about 44 = quarter note, but feeling it in two half note beats.

The *sarabande* (Spanish: *zarabanda*) was a dance that may have originated in Mexico. Evidently Carré's version was known by Sanz, who transcribed it into Italian tablature and included it in his 1674 book (book I, plate 12, *Zarabanda francesa*). Like the *allemande*, the *sarabande* too was slowed down by the French. James Talbot described the French version in about 1690 as, "a soft passionate Movement, always set in a slow Triple . . . apt to move the Passions and to disturb the tranquility of the Mind." That sounds like a pretty tall order, but whether or not one is fully able to capture the mood, I suggest playing the piece at a tempo of about 76 = quarter note.

Carré uses only one ornament sign in the *Allemande* and *Sarabande*—an ×. He doesn't specify which ornament the sign represents, but based on musical context and comparing his use of it with that of Francesco Corbetta, who also published a guitar book in Paris in 1671, it seems to be an upper note trill, which Corbetta called a *tremblement*. Make sure to extend the trill at cadence points, such as at bars 6 and 14. The rapid thirty-second notes after the trills should be played in the French manner by brushing the right-hand index finger down across the top two courses and ending on the downbeat of the next bar with the middle finger. Make sure to strum the chords in a controlled and gentle manner.

A facsimile edition of Carré's *Livre de Guitarre contenant plusieurs pieces* ... (Paris, 1671), published by Minkoff (Geneva, 1977), is available from OMI.

Editorial

The only correction made to the original tablatures is in the third beat of bar 3 of the *Sarabande,* where I have made the original letter f on the third course an h. I added repeat signs and made first and second endings to both the *Allemande* and *Sarabande* to clarify their musical structure. In the transcriptions, I used violin bow markings to indicate the down strums.

Allemande–Sarabande

Antoine Carré

Livre de Guitarre (Paris, 1671), 13–14

Antoine Carré, *Allemande–Sarabande*

10

PIECES SUITABLE FOR STRINGING B

PRELUD[IO]-CHIACONA—FRANCESCO CORBETTA (1648)

A much-travelled native of Pavia, Italy, Francesco Corbetta (ca. 1615–81) was one of the most influential guitarists of the seventeenth century. Throughout his life, he managed to win the support of powerful patrons, including two kings, Charles II of England and France's Louis XIV. His several published guitar books were well known throughout Europe, beginning with his first, published in Bologna in 1639. The present pieces are from his fourth book, *Varii scherzi di sonate per la chitara spagnola,* which was published in Brussels in 1648 and dedicated to Archduke Leopold Wilhelm of Austria, then Regent of the Spanish Netherlands. There is no record of Corbetta's ever having held a post at the Regent's court in the Netherlands, so perhaps the dedication was made in the hopes of securing one.

The *Prelud[io] al 5to tuono* (in the fifth mode; that is, the Lydian mode in Renaissance music theory, transposed by Corbetta to C) is a delicate, free-style, introductory piece. As it would go against the character of a prelude to perform it with a steady beat throughout, the player is encouraged to speed up or slow down certain passages. For example, where the texture is lacy with many upper notes, speed up to suggest a burst of emotion. Or slow down for passages that seem to suggest that a thoughtful, lingering feeling is wanted.

The piece opens with a nice flourish of *campanelas* in the first bar and a rapid series of slurs in the second, which should steady by bar 3. In order to emphasize the pungent discords in the middle of bar 5 and in beats 2 and 3 of bar 20, the chords should be spread, even the ones comprising just two notes. Bars 11–12, which involve a sequence of 7–6 chords, should be spread as well; likewise the 4–3 cadence at the end of bar 22. In the final bar, a gentle down-strum combined with an extended main note trill on the second course is effective.

Two ornament signs are used. The first is ✗, which Corbetta calls *tremolo* but doesn't explain how it is executed. Based on musical context, he seems to be calling for a main note trill in some places and an upper note trill in others, while in one or two other spots he wants a quick lower mordent. Corbetta, like numerous other contemporary guitar composers, appears to be leaving the specific choice of ornament up to the player. The second sign is **x**, called by Corbetta *tremolo sforzato,* or *accento,* by which he clearly means vibrato.

Corbetta's *Chiacona* (Italian, usually *ciaccona* or *ciacona;* Spanish, *chacona*) is quite different in character from the slightly later French *chaconne,* and exceedingly different from J. S. Bach's eighteenth-century chaconne. The *ciaccona* began life in the late sixteenth century, possibly in Mexico, as a lively, suggestive dance-song, traditionally accompanied by guitar and castanets. It soon was taken up by the Italians and, from 1606 through the late seventeenth century, one or more *ciacconi* could be found in every *alfabeto* guitar book, published or manuscript. Musically, it's a four or eight bar harmonic pattern or ground, always in triple time and in the major mode, and often with a progression of I-V-vi-V (filled out with intermediary harmonies). Corbetta's version follows this pattern with a chain of units in eight-bar groups presenting harmonic, rhythmic, and melodic variations. Although today the appearance of three half notes in a bar immediately suggests a somewhat slow tempo, for players in Corbetta's time it suggested the quick three-quarter time waltz tempo of a later period, or half note = 112.

A key stylistic feature of the *ciaccona* is the *hemiola,* a shifting of the accent from three to a broad two in or across certain bars. It is found most often in the two bars before a cadence; in the present piece, however, it makes its first appearance near the beginning at bars 2–3, where the stress occurs on the first and third beats of bar 2 and the second beat of bar 3. The *hemiola* should be emphasized, and for that reason I have placed editorial accent marks in the tablature wherever one occurs. In bars 24–27, syncopations in the melody are called for and thus are similarly marked. The accents should be played somewhat subtly, not hammered out. Bar 51 seems to call for an upper octave g' on the third quarter note. (See the commentary that precedes Sanz's *Pavanas* for a reminder of how to deal with an upper octave g'.) For the strummed chords, Corbetta's tablature implies that an *alfabeto* chord should include all five courses in the stroke, while the partial chords with stroke signs probably mean selective chord voicing. (See the transcription for my interpretation of the latter.) Other markings are the double diagonal lines that separate the sections. Corbetta sometimes places them at eight-bar intervals and sometimes at four.

To set the character of the piece and contrast it with the lightness and delicacy of the *Preludio,* I suggest playing the opening sections, bars 1–20, in a strong, expansive manner. Bars 21 to the downbeat of 32 can be a bit lighter to bring out the sudden change of texture and the more delicate syncopations of bars 24–27. Play strongly and broadly again at bars 32 to the downbeat of 36; then, like an echoed reply, more quietly to the downbeat of bar 40. From that point through bar 55, it is essential to remain pianissimo in order to allow the transparent, bell-like notes to ping out and to savor the discords that are produced. To maximize the effect, use *tenuto* technique, holding down every note and chord for as long as possible so that the notes ring on into each other. This effect can be spellbinding if executed properly. Make a crescendo into bar 56. From that point to the downbeat of bar 64 there is what appears to be a succession of rather simple strummed chords. This section cries out for rhythmic embellishment in the form of strongly played *repicci* (described in part 1, chapter 5 under the heading Rhythmic Ornamentation). The piece ends with a rhythmic cascade of slurred notes (discussed and explained in part 1, chapter 6 under the heading Performance Markings).

A facsimile edition of Corbetta's *Varii scherzi di sonata per la chitara spagnola . . .* (Brussels, 1648), published by Archivum Musicum (Florence, 1983), is available from OMI.

Editorial

Chiacona: Bar 6, third beat quarter note on third course changed from number 3 to 2. Bar 32, original number 3 eliminated on the fifth course in the second beat chord because it is unusual and awkward, and because its pitch is already present. Bar 44, incorrect number 0 was eliminated from the third course, last beat. Accent marks have been placed in the tablature wherever a *hemiola* occurs. In bars 24–27, syncopations in the melody are called for and are similarly marked. Asterisks have been placed under the notes in the tablature where the music seems to suggest that the upper octave string and the bourdon should be played together; if there are no asterisks, play only the upper octave.

Prelud[io]

Francesco Corbetta

Varii scherzi di sonate per la chitarra spagnola (Brussels, 1648), 32–33

Chiacona

Francesco Corbetta

Varii scherzi di sonate per la chitarra spagnola (Brussels, 1648), 28–31

Francesco Corbetta, *Prelud[io]–Chiacona*

55

Prelud[io]–Chiacona

ALEMANDA–CORRENTE–SARABANDA–GIGA—
GIOVANNI BATTISTA GRANATA (1674)

A local guitar teacher and occasional "extra musician" in Bologna's famed Concerto Palatino, Giovanni Battista Granata (ca. 1622–87)—whose day job was that of a barber-surgeon licensed to deal not only with hair but also with minor medical procedures—was also a prolific composer. Seven collections of his music were published between 1646 and 1684. The present suite in the key of D major is from his fifth book, *Novi capricci armonici musicali . . .* (Bologna, 1674).

All four items in Granata's suite are dance forms, beginning with an *alemanda*. Unlike the French *allemande* of the time, the *alemanda* was still regarded as a dance form by some Italian composers. In performing pieces named for dances, it is important to know the character of the dances even if the pieces weren't actually meant to be danced to, because the name of the dance is often a clue to the tempo that the composer had in mind. To evoke the moderately paced ceremonial character of Granata's *Alemanda*, I suggest a tempo of half note = 60.

The nature of the Italian *corrente* was discussed in the commentary to Valdambrini's version. The name of the dance means running or flowing, and Granata's *Corrente* does just that. It begins with a run of *campanelas*—a textural feature he employs throughout—which should be played at a tempo of quarter note = 138 to advance the flowing movement of the piece. Note that there are several places where an upper octave g' is needed on the third course: bars 2, 4, 9, 10, 11, 15, 17, 22, and 23.

The Italian *sarabanda* of Granata's time still retained a moderately quick tempo, reflecting its Spanish origins as the *zarabanda;* but it, too, was being slowed down as a dance form (albeit not as radically as the French *sarabande*). Try to evoke a feeling of poise and stateliness. A tempo of about quarter note = 76 would be appropriate. A third course upper g' seems to be called for only in bars 9, 21, and 29.

The *giga,* like the English jig, was the fastest dance of the time. It's usually notated in $\frac{6}{8}$ or, to save having to write out so many bar lines, its multiple of $\frac{12}{8}$. Granata's is in duple time, which, as far as the actual dance steps are concerned, equates to the $\frac{12}{8}$ versions. Its pulse should correspond to half-bar units with a tempo of half note = approximately 54, or even faster if one's technique is up to it. The dance is one that skips along briskly, which is why it was sometimes associated with or called a *saltarello*. The present *Giga* provides a lively, virtuoso finale to the suite.

Only two ornament signs are used throughout the suite: **T** (*tremolo*) for a main note trill and # for vibrato.

A facsimile edition of Granata's *Novi capricci armonici musicali . . .* (Bologna, 1674), published by Forni (Bologna, 2005), is available from OMI.

Editorial

Alemanda: Bar 12, the *alfabeto* **I** chord changed to **F.** I have added asterisks to indicate which fourth course notes should include the bourdon, and a cross in bars 8, 19, and 21 to indicate that an upper octave g' is needed on the third course.

Corrente: I have added a + sign in bars 2, 4, 9, 10, 11, 15, 17, 22, and 23 to indicate that an upper octave g' is needed on the third course.

Sarabanda: Bar 17, last note changed from 3 to 4. Bar 24, end of second beat, original number 4 misplaced on second course changed to fifth course. I have added a + sign in bars 9, 21, and 29 to indicate that an upper octave g' is needed on the third course.

Giga: Bar 1, end of third beat, misplaced 2 on third course changed to second course. Bar 4, beginning of third beat, misplaced 7 on fourth course changed to fifth course.

All first and second time bars in the suite are editorial.

Alemanda–Corrente–Sarabande–Giga

Giovanni Battista Granata

Novi capricci armonici musicali (Bologna, 1674), 40–43

1. Alemanda

2. Corrente

3. Sarabanda

4. *Giga*

Giovanni Battista Granata, *Alemanda–Corrente–Sarabanda–Giga*

1. *Alemanda*

2. *Corrente*

3. Sarabanda

4. Giga

PASSACAILLE DITE MARIONA—LELIO COLISTA (CA. 1675)

The renowned lutenist and guitarist Lelio Colista (1629–80) of Rome was also a celebrated composer. His works include instrumental ensemble music, oratorios, arias, and cantatas. From the late 1650s to ca. 1665, his patron was the powerful Cardinal Flavio Chigi, a nephew of Pope Alexander VII. During this period Colista was a member of the cardinal's entourage accompanying him on diplomatic missions to other European courts. He worked with many important musicians of the day, including Pasquini and Stradella, and his ensemble once included the young Corelli, who acknowledged Colista's influence. Gaspar Sanz studied with Colista in Rome and said that he learned a great deal from him. Contemporaries throughout Europe, including Henry Purcell, regarded him as one of the best composers of his time.

The *Passacaille dite Mariona* (Passacaglia called Mariona) is found in a guitar manuscript now in the Conservatoire Royal de Musique in Brussels (MS 5.615). Compiled in the early eighteenth century by a local cleric, Jean Baptiste de Castillion (1680–1753), this manuscript is an anthology of some of the best music of the previous century. The *mariona,* a popular Spanish dance, was particularly associated with theatrical productions. It apparently had more freedom in its movements and gestures than many of the more straitlaced dances of the period. Like the *ciaccona,* the music for the *passacaille* is based on a repeated harmonic pattern or ground. Colista's *mariona* version, which uses a I-V-vi-IV-V harmonic scheme, is both a high-spirited dance piece and, with its bold, infectious rhythms, syncopations, and ingenious variations, a joyful demonstration of the baroque guitar's many resources.

Although Colista's original was undoubtedly written in Italian tablature, Castillion "translated" the piece into French tablature for his own use; the ornament signs are French-style as well. His ornament signs, **x** (*tremblement*) and ⁾ (*mortellement*) are not explained, but they probably indicate an upper note trill and a descending appoggiatura, respectively. I suggest substituting the Italian-style main note trill and lower mordent, which Colista almost certainly intended. The vertical line under the chords in bars 5 and 21 indicates that they should be played with a stroke of the thumb alone. This technique produces a different, contrasting sound to the one produced by the normal strokes played with the backs of the nails.

For tempo, I suggest a lively, quarter note = 120. The following dynamic scheme can be used effectively: from bar 1 to the first beat of bar 12, *forte;* then, to emphasize the sudden change in texture, *piano;* followed by a crescendo in bars 18–19, building to *forte* on the first beat of bar 20. From the second beat of bar 28, *piano,* to highlight the string of *campanelas;* but at the second beat of bar 36, *forte.* From the second beat of bar 44, *mezzoforte,* but crescendo in bars 50–51, building to *forte* on the first beat of bar 52. After the first beat of bar 60, *mezzoforte* until the first beat of bar 72; then *forte* until the end of the piece. The *campanela* and slur passages, especially the final one, should be played with as much panache as possible.

The Castillion manuscript (sometimes known as the Le Cocq manuscript), was published in facsimile by Éditions Culture et Civilisation (Brussels, 1979), but it is now out of print.

Editorial

Bar 41: first beat, a misplaced letter *a* on the fifth course has been changed to the fourth course. Bar 48: second sixteenth note, a misplaced *a* on the fourth course has been changed to the fifth course. The diagonal lines are original and are used to separate sections.

The usual editorial asterisks and crosses indicate the use of a bourdon on the fourth course and an upper octave g' on the third course, respectively. I also have added accent marks in the places where a *hemiola* or note should be emphasized. In bars 24, 28, 68, and 72, the editorial dots on the staves indicate selective chord voicing.

Passacaille dite Mariona

Lelio Colista

Brussels, Conservatoire Royal de Musique, MS 5.615, 116–17

67

Passacaille dite Mariona (continued)

68

Lelio Colista, *Passacaille dite Mariona*

69

PRELUDE—ANGELO MICHELE BARTOLOTTI (CA. 1655)

Bartolotti (ca. 1615–81) is arguably one of the foremost guitar composers of the Baroque period. A native of Bologna, he was a member of an ensemble of Italian musicians at the Stockholm court of Queen Christina of Sweden, who also had a similar French ensemble. Upon Christina's abdication in 1654 he traveled to Innsbruck, where he found employment at the Habsburg court of Archduke Ferdinand Karl, whose choirmaster was the renowned composer Antonio Cesti.

From his very first publication (Florence, 1640), it was clear that Bartolotti was way ahead of his contemporaries—including Corbetta, whose own modest first collection had appeared a year earlier. In his second book, published in Rome ca. 1655, he demonstrated an understanding and mastery of the guitar's unique idioms that went unequaled until much later in the century. He dedicated it to Queen Christina, who, by this date, resided there. Many titles of pieces, including the present *Prelude,* are in French, reflecting, perhaps, the Queen's tastes.

As its title implies, much of the *Prelude* should be played without a fixed tempo. It begins with an arpeggiated flourish immediately followed by dramatic scale sequences. The latter should be played in a free rhythm, the notes flowing seamlessly one into the next and building to a stronger, second arpeggiated flourish that ends in the dominant of the key at bar 11. The next section, beginning at bar 12, is fugal in nature and uses two-part contrapuntal writing. It should be played at a steady tempo of approximately quarter note = 100, but remember to feel and play the beat in two; that is, half note beat = 50. (This practice was discussed in the commentary to Gaspar Sanz's *Pavanas*.) Slow down a bit at the cadence point in bars 23–24 in preparation for the third section, which starts at bar 25. Here begins a *gigue*-like section in compound triple meter. Following tradition, a proportional feeling must be maintained between the two sections, so keep to the same tempo, but now with a beat of dotted quarter note = 50.

The next section, beginning at bar 45, returns to duple meter with forceful, driving sixteenth notes played at the previous tempo and a beat of half note = 50. Maintaining this tempo might pose something of technical challenge; if so, take it a bit slower. However, starting at bar 57, it is essential to be at maximum tempo for the final torrent of notes in *campanelas* before coming to a peaceful resolution on the final D major chord.

For the music in this publication, Bartolotti's instructions reveal that his ⚡ sign means an arpeggio. He doesn't explain how to play it, but given the style of the piece, it probably requires a rapid, free tempo with a rolling back and forth of the notes for dramatic effect. Another of his ornament signs is ⸲, which he calls a *trillo,* but which, to judge by the diagram he provides to show how to play it (starting on a note above the written note, then quickly pulling off it to the written note) proves to be a descending appoggiatura! His *x* sign indicates a *mordente,* which begins on the written note, rapidly slurs down to the note below, then back up to the written note (like a modern lower mordent). The slanted lines linking notes in the bass or treble are his *tenuto* markings, which indicate that the initial note of the group should be held while the others are played.

A facsimile edition of Bartolotti's *Secondo libro di chitarra* . . . (Rome, ca. 1655) along with his *Primo libro di chitarra spagnola* . . . (Florence, 1640), published by Minkoff (Geneva, 1984), is available from OMI.

Editorial

The original tablature is remarkably accurate with only a redundant number 3 on the fourth course of the last beat of bar 47, which I have eliminated. I added the arpeggio sign in bar 11, because that bar is similar to bar 1 in which Bartolotti included an arpeggio. I added the usual * sign to indicate the use of a bourdon on the fourth course, and + sign to indicate an upper octave g' on the third course.

Prelude

Angelo Michele Bartolotti

Secondo libro di Chitarra (Rome, ca. 1655), 69–70

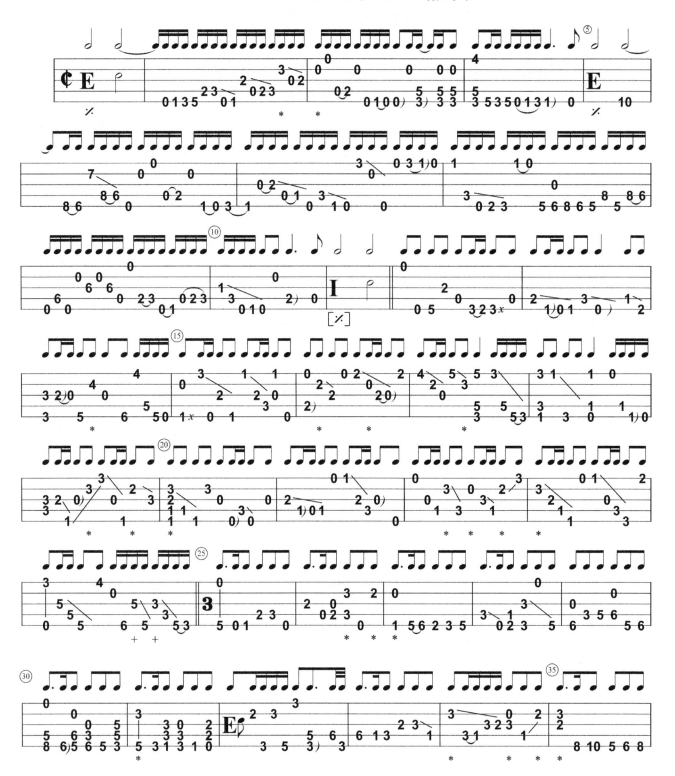

Prelude

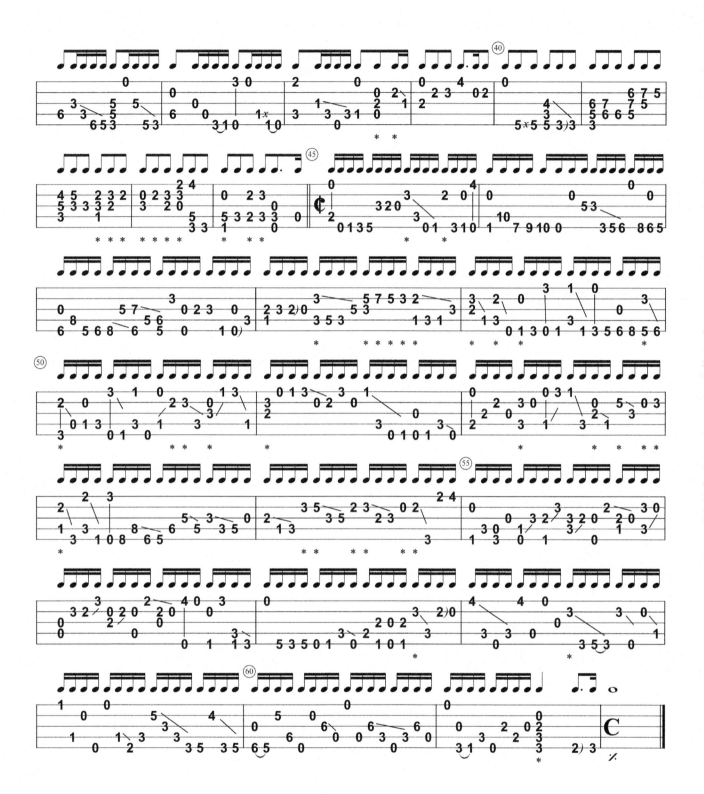

73

Angelo Michele Bartolotti, *Prelude*

ALLEMANDE "LA FURIEUSE"—FRANÇOIS CAMPION (1705)

François Campion (ca. 1685–1747) was one of two theorbo players in the orchestra of the Académie Royale de Musique from 1704 to 1719 and probably played continuo for many of the operas performed there during that period. He was also the composer of two collections of French *airs,* which were published in 1719 and 1734 respectively. Several of his *airs* were selected for inclusion in anthology publications. In addition, he was a renowned teacher of guitar and theorbo in Paris and published a highly influential treatise on continuo playing in 1716 and additions to it in 1730. He published only one book of guitar solos, *Nouvelles découvertes sur la Guitarre* (Paris, 1705), but continued to add further pieces to his own printed copy in manuscript over the next several years.

Employing late Baroque style and techniques combined with some manifestations of the newer *galant* and early Classical styles, Campion composed guitar music of exceptional quality and charm. Many pieces in the book call for various scordatura tunings, but those in the final section are for the normal tuning, including his *Allemande "La Furieuse."* As its title implies, this is a descriptive piece in the form of an *allemande* that evokes the actions of an impetuous woman—or perhaps, depending on how it's played, a crazy one. The music alternates between the formal, controlled movements of the stately French *allemande* and the unexpected outbursts of rapid, virtuoso scale passages that represent *"La Furieuse,"* as she disrupts the dignified mood. The piece seems to call for a not too strict tempo, perhaps employing some degree of rubato, and the scale passages should be played as rapidly as possible.

Campion doesn't explain his ornament signs, but his use of an *x* with a small, auxiliary tablature letter above it can be interpreted as an upper note trill with its beginning pitch specified by the small tablature letter. He uses a $^)$ sign in bar 13, which, given the musical context, should probably be played as an ascending appoggiatura. Bar 14 is a cadence point requiring an extended upper note trill; the release of the trill should be played with the right-hand index finger brushing across the first and second courses. Although these two notes are shown as sixteenth notes, taking into account musical context, they should probably be played as thirty-second notes. The vertical line between the notes in bar 5 means that they should be played simultaneously, not separated. The diagonal *tenuto* lines in bars 25, 31, 32, and 33 are Campion's own. The dots on the staves in bars 19 and 26 for selective chord voicing are also his original markings, as is the dynamic change, *doucement* (softly), called for in bar 28.

A facsimile edition of Campion's *Nouvelles découvertes sur la guitarre* (Paris, 1705), including his manuscript additions, published by Minkoff (Geneva, 1977), and of his printed book alone by Performer's Facsimiles (New York, 1993), are available from OMI.

Editorial

Rhythmic misprints in the original have been corrected and appear in the tablature between square brackets. My asterisks indicate which fourth course notes I believe should include the bourdon. The first and second endings are editorial. As mentioned above, the dots on the staves in bars 19 and 26 to indicate selective chord voicing are Campion's, while the others are editorial suggestions.

Allemande "La Furieuse"

François Campion

Nouvelles découvertes sur la Guitarre (Paris, 1705), 41–42

Allemande "La Furieuse" (continued)

François Campion, *Allemande "La Furieuse"*

79

FOLIES D'ESPAGNE—FRANÇOIS LE COCQ (CA. 1700)

The music of Flemish guitarist François Le Cocq (fl. 1676–1729) is found entirely in a manuscript copied by his friend, Jean Baptiste de Castillion (Brussels, Conservatoire Royal de Musique, MS 5.615; see also the commentary to Lelio Colista's *Passacaille dite Marionas* above.) Le Coq presented the pieces to Castillion in 1729, by which time the composer was elderly and had retired. Hardly anything is known of his life save Castillion's brief account in the manuscript. He was a musician in the Chapel Royal in Brussels and guitar teacher to the wife of the Elector of Bavaria—possibly Adelaida of Savoy (1636–76), a renowned patron of music in Munich, also known for an earlier manuscript of guitar music that belonged to her, now housed in the Bavarian National Library (Mus. Ms. 1522, ca. 1660). Le Cocq's music was never published, yet it was definitely known by the Spanish guitarist, Santiago de Murcia, who re-worked some of the pieces and claimed them as his own.

Like the *pavaniglia* (*pavanas*) and *ciaccona* (*chiacona*) in the versions by Sanz and Corbetta (described above), the *folia* is a harmonic chord pattern used for variations. It originated in sixteenth-century Spain, though Le Cocq's version follows one of the later types—a basic i-V-i-VII-III-VII-i-V (with repeat) pattern—which first appeared in France in the mid-seventeenth century. His *Folies d'Espagne,* a set of twenty-two variations comprising many of the guitar's characteristic idioms, can be used as both a thorough workout for the development of right- and left-hand technique and an impressive, show-stopping performance piece.

Several contrasting tempos and moods are recommended. Nos. 1–3 can be played at a steady tempo of quarter note = 88. Note that no. 2 begins with a dotted rhythm pattern for the first two bars, and then continues with straight eighth notes. It appears likely that this change was effected merely to eliminate the tedium of having to write out the dotted pattern, so I would suggest ignoring the straight eighth notes and continuing to play the dotted rhythm pattern. Nos. 4–7 can be played a bit faster to give a sense of a new movement and a change in style. No. 8 is specifically marked "adagio" by Le Cocq, so play it at a tempo similar to the first three. No. 9 switches to an allegro at the change into $\frac{9}{8}$ meter; perhaps play it dotted quarter note = 120, making sure that the eighth notes are played like triplets. No. 10 switches back to $\frac{3}{4}$ meter and should slow in tempo in order to prepare for the next variation. At a tempo of about quarter note = at least 104, no. 11 gets flashy with its rapid sixteenth note scales alternating with *repicci*. In an effort to avoid having to write out every single fast note, Le Coq (or Castillion) used a dotted half note to stand in for the *repicci* after the first three bars. Ignore the dotted half note and continue to play the *repicci*.

At no. 12, we encounter a study in thirds, wherein the normal sixteen-bar variation is expanded to thirty-two. A study in slurs follows at no. 13. The initial chords should be strummed boldly and dramatically, and the slurs played as rapidly as possible. The chords in nos. 14 and 15 are marked entirely as down strokes with dots over them, suggesting that they're to be played allegro and staccato in a quite dramatic fashion. Next we arrive at a study in arpeggios. Each bar in no. 16 begins with a down stroke followed by arpeggios in triplets. The arpeggios change to a pattern of straight, rolling eighth notes in the treble range at no. 17.

Nos. 18 and 19 begin in duple time until the final two bars of each, which go back to triple time (three quarter notes). The duple time sections should be played at a tempo of half note = 60 so they're in proportion to the quarter note = 120 of the final two bars of triple time. By maintaining this relationship, the rolling arpeggios that follow the strong initial down strokes in both variations surge forth in a thrilling torrent of notes. After the first two bars of no. 18, Le Cocq again reverts to an abbreviated style of notation to save having to write out so many notes; the player, however, should continue the pattern of the first two bars. Similarly, the dotted half note stroke signs in these duple time bars are not meant to be taken literally; they merely indicate the *direction* of the strokes.

No. 20 continues at a tempo of 120, but the style changes from arpeggios to *repicci* for the remainder of the piece. No. 20, at this speed, results in a slow *repicco* after the initial down stroke. In no. 21, the *repicco* pattern becomes more complicated and intense. And in no. 22, it gets downright strenuous, with a final section of rapid-fire *repicci* on every single beat. If executed properly, at its conclusion the player will need to lie down and rest for a few minutes.

The Castillion manuscript (also known as the Le Cocq manuscript), was published in facsimile by Éditions Culture et Civilisation (Brussels, 1979), but is now out of print.

Editorial

Le Cocq repeats the time signatures at the beginning of every variation, but for the sake of a cleaner-looking score, I have not followed suit. The duple-time signatures in nos. 18 and 19 are editorial. I have made the stroke signs in the tablature smaller than in previous pieces in order to save space. The accent marks that appear at certain cadence points have been added to emphasize a *hemiola* pattern. The dot on the staff in bar 36 that signals selective chord voicing is original. I have added dots elsewhere in the tablature for the same purpose. The abbreviated form of notation found in the last three variations is editorial and follows the style of Le Cocq's in nos. 11 and 18.

Folies d'Espagne

François Le Cocq

Brussels, Conservatoire Royal de Musique, MS 5.615, 74–81

82

Folies d'Espagne (continued)

86

François Le Cocq, *Folies d'Espagne*

90

Folies d'Espagne

93

11

PIECES SUITABLE FOR STRINGING C

PAVANIGLIA CON PARTI VARIATE— GIOVANNI PAOLO FOSCARINI (CA. 1630)

The *Pavaniglia con parti variate* (Pavaniglia with variation sections) is from *Il primo, secondo, e terzo libro della chitarra spagnola . . .* (The First, Second, and Third Books for Spanish Guitar) by "L'Academico Caliginoso detto Il Furioso" (a member of the Accademia dei Caliginosi, a literary and music society founded in Ancona in 1624, whose nickname at the Academy was "Il Furioso"). In addition to not naming its author, the book also carries no place or year of publication; ca. 1630 seems a reasonable guess.

In his next (fourth) book, which appeared in around 1632, Il Furioso's identity is revealed on the title page as Giovanni Paolo Foscarini. Like his previous and subsequent books, it is cumulative in nature; for example, his fourth book, in addition to the new material, also contained the music from his earlier three publications! He apparently engraved the music plates for his books himself and took them with him wherever he went to live and work.

From his various publications, we learn that before he went to Ancona, Foscarini, describing himself as a musician and player of the lute and theorbo, worked in Brussels at the court of the Austrian Archduke Albert Ernst (1559–1621) and his wife Isabella Clara Eugenia, the sister of Philip III of Spain, who acted as governors of the Spanish Netherlands. The Flemish artist and humanist scholar Peter Paul Rubens and the Italian virtuoso violinist and composer Biagio Marini were also members of their court.

Foscarini's third book, *Il primo, secondo, e terzo libro della chitarra spagnola* of ca. 1630, more than hints at a connection with Verona. Here one finds an engraved portrait (not by Foscarini) and a verse in praise of him by Oratio Abbaco, a "gentilhuomo Veronese," as well as a piece dedicated to Count Paolo Canossa of Verona, a guitar aficionado to whom the huge manuscript of *alfabeto* solos and songs by the guitarist Francesco Palumbi (Verona, Biblioteca Civica, Ms. 1434) was also dedicated.

To judge by the dedications of pieces in his fourth book to such Roman notables as four members of the Orsini family—Alessandro, Flavio, Virginio, and Paolo Giordano II, the Duke of Bracciano—by the time of its publication in ca. 1632, Foscarini was a free-lance musician living in Rome. Other dedicatees, who apparently studied guitar with him, were the prominent Roman painters the Cavaliere d'Arpino (Giuseppe Cesari) and Fabio della Corgna, as well as members of the Borghese family. Later editions of his books have various dedication dates of 1638 (Rome), 1640 (Rome), 1644 (Rome), and 1649 (Venice).

The nature of the *pavaniglia* has already been described in the commentary to Gaspar Sanz's *Pavanas.* However, Foscarini based his variations on an earlier version of the ground, which, in addition to its characteristic harmonic pattern, also has a distinctive melodic profile. His setting is entirely in the *pizzicato* (lute) style without any strummed chords. He includes three different styles of guitar music in his ca. 1630 book: strictly *alfabeto* chords (*battuto* style), lute style, and a mixture of two. The mixed style appears for the first time in this book, and it might very well have been Foscarini's invention, which was later adopted by nearly all of the best guitar composers. In his preface, he says that of the pieces (*sonate*) called "*Pizzicate*, I will not say so much, having put them here more for the interest (*abbellimento*) of the book than for anything else since I well know that they are more appropriate for the lute than for the guitar. . . ." This explanation underscores the fact that a major feature of guitar technique was the strumming of chords. That being said, since the present *Pavaniglia* is written in lute style and is likely for stringing C, it can be played on a classical guitar without in any way misrepresenting the music.

Like Sanz's *Pavanas,* Foscarini's *Pavaniglia* should be taken at a tempo of approximately half note = 60. The first sixteen bars present a clear statement of the harmonic pattern and its characteristic melody. Be sure to hold down as many of the first notes in the bars as possible (*tenuto*), and continue to do so for the three variations that follow. Foscarini uses no ornament signs in this piece, but that doesn't mean no ornaments should be added, simply that he's leaving it up to the player to add them where he or she sees fit. Indeed, his instructions in the preface to the book mention the following ornaments: *tremolo* (main note trill), *strascini* (slurs), and vibrato. Ornaments added by the player should be on one of the two half note beats in the bar, usually the first (strongest).

A facsimile edition of Foscarini's fifth book, *Li cinque libri della chitarra alla spagnola . . .* (Rome, 1640), which also includes all of the music from his previous books, was published by Archivium Musicum (Florence, 1979), and is available from OMI.

Editorial

There are several misprints in the original tablature. Bar 3, second and third quarter notes, numbers 2 and 0 on fourth course corrected to 2 and 0 on the fifth course. Bar 15, third quarter note on third course given as number 3, corrected to 4. Bar 29, second quarter note on fourth course given as number 5, corrected to 3; third quarter note on third course given as number 3, corrected to 4. Bar 31, second quarter note on third course corrected to fourth course. Bar 44, third quarter note beat on third course corrected to fourth course.

The time signature is editorial.

Pavaniglia con parti variate

Giovanni Paolo Foscarini

Il primo, secondo, e terzo libro della chitarra (n.l., ca. 1630), Book III, 39

Pavaniglia con parti variate

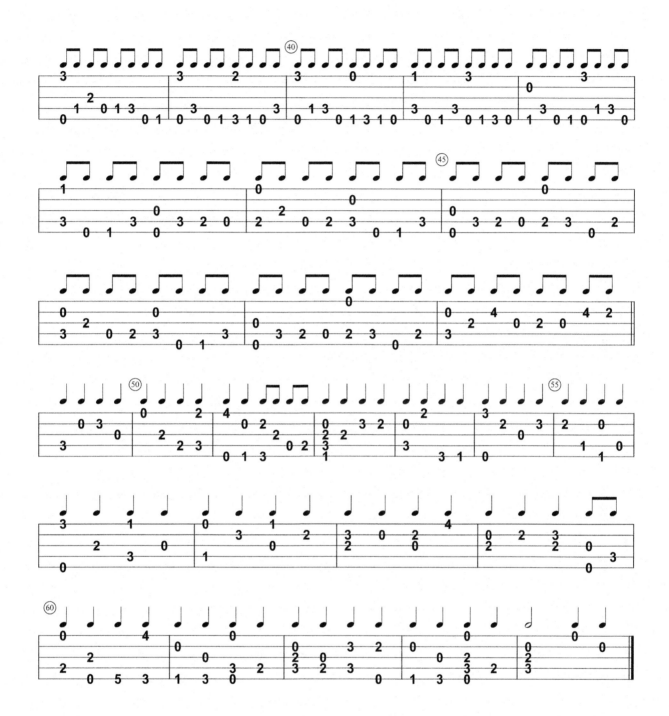

Giovanni Paolo Foscarini, *Pavaniglia con parti variate*

ARIA DI FIORENZA—ANONYMOUS/
CARLO CALVI (COMPILER) (1646)

This piece is from a collection of guitar solos by two "Eccellenti Professori," whose names its compiler-editor, Carlo Calvi, neglected to mention. The first portion of the book contains *alfabeto* solos for a presumably smaller sized, five-course guitar called a *chitarriglia,* and the second for a normal sized *chitarra.* The latter portion consists entirely of music in the *pizzicato* (lute) style. It is known that some of the prefatory information and several of the *alfabeto* solos are adaptations of material found in Francesco Corbetta's 1639 book, but the *pizzicato*-style pieces have not been found elsewhere.

The *Aria di Fiorenza* is an arrangement for guitar of a piece composed by Emilio de' Cavaliere for the magnificent Medici wedding celebrations that took place in Florence in 1589. The festivities included a spectacular musical production, which culminated in a *ballo;* that is, a stage work with singing as well as dancing. The *ballo* involved a huge cast, including three solo singers, two of whom accompanied themselves on large and small guitars, and it had a memorable harmonic theme—the *Aria di Fiorenza*—which soon became the musical emblem of Florence. It is found in nearly every guitar book from the late sixteenth through the mid-seventeenth century, as well as in countless versions for other instruments.

Unlike other harmonic patterns, such as the *pavaniglia, ciacona, mariona,* and *folia* (discussed above), the *Aria di Fiorenza* has an extended 42-bar scheme divided into five 8-bar sections, each of which can be repeated. Although its length allows for a considerable number of increasingly complex variations, the setting in Calvi's collection is quite basic—which means the player is expected to improvise on the material that's given.

I suggest a tempo of half note = 88 in the duple time sections and a dotted half note = 88 in the triple time sections, which means that a bar of duple time lasts exactly the same length of time as a bar in triple time. There are no ornament signs in the original; however, the player is expected to add his or her own main note trills, slurs, and vibrato. To make the structure of the piece as clear as possible, I have headed each of the five sections A, B, C, D, and E. The first A section in duple time is followed by a written-out varied repeat marked A'. The triple time portion is, of course, the same material but in a different meter.

A facsimile edition of Calvi's *Intavolatura di chitarra, e chitarriglia . . .* (Bologna, 1646), published by Archivium Musicum (Florence, 1980), is available from OMI.

Editorial

There are a few misprints in the original. Bar 28, first beat, the numbers 3 on the first course and 2 on the second were corrected to 2 and 3, respectively. Bar 72, the last quarter note, given as number 3, was corrected to 2. Bar 81, first beat, number 3 on the second course was corrected to 5.

The double bar lines separating sections, the first and second endings, and the time signatures are all editorial.

Aria di Fiorenza

Anonymous/
Carlo Calvi (compiler)

Intavolatura di chitarra, e chitarriglia (Bologna, 1646), 28–29

Aria di Fiorenza

Anonymous/Carlo Calvi (compiler), *Aria di Fiorenza*

104

CAPRICCIO–SARABANDA–CAPRICCIO—
FRANCESCO ASIOLI (1676)

A resident of Reggio, near Modena, Asioli dedicated his first guitar book of 1674 to his patron, Francesco II d'Este, Duke of Modena and Reggio. His second work, presumably another guitar book, is lost, but his third, *Concerti armonici per la chitarra spagnuola,* which includes the present pieces, was published in Bologna two years after his first and is dedicated to the Collegio de Nobili di Parma (Fellowship of Noblemen of Parma), the confraternity for which he was apparently the resident guitar teacher. Each of the forty-eight pieces in the collection is dedicated to a specific member of the confraternity, mainly counts, barons, marquises, and abbots.

The first *Capriccio,* the *Sarabanda,* and the second *Capriccio* are the last items in the book. I have combined them to form a suite even though none of the pieces in the collection are organized in this manner. The first of the *capricci,* written entirely in *pizzicato* style, is a quite cheerful and charming piece. As its name implies, it should be played capriciously, or freely, with no set tempo. I suggest playing the sixteenth-note scales fairly rapidly in both sections until they reach their high points. In the first section, there are two such places, and I have indicated the first with a short fermata and the second with a longer one. In the second section, I suggest dashing headlong through the sixteenth notes, taking care, however, to make a slight separation before the last beat of bar 8 and the last beat of bar 12. The ornament signs in the tablature, **T** and ♮, stand for *tremolo* (main note trill) and vibrato respectively, although Asioli does not explain the signs in his preface.

The *Sarabanda* is presented in the Italian manner, as a dance form, and should be played at a steady tempo of about quarter note = 80 throughout. Try to convey a sense of simplicity, grace, and elegance. The piece opens with one bar in *battuto* (strummed) style, while the remainder is in *pizzicato* style. If one's guitar isn't strung with an upper octave on the third course, one can play the third eighth note g in bar 15 on the second course at the eighth fret and slur down to the seventh.

The second *Capriccio,* like the first, should be played with no set tempo until bar 6, where it changes to triple meter. As this is a dance-like section, it should be kept at a steady beat with a tempo of about quarter note = 120. I have added accent marks in bars 16–17 as a reminder to emphasize the *hemiola* rhythm. If desired, it is possible to make a repeat of this section by going back to the eighth note of bar 6.

There is no facsimile edition of Asioli's *Concerti armonici per la chitarra spagnuola* . . . (Bologna, 1676).

Editorial

I have corrected the following misprints in the original:

First *Capriccio:* Bar 5, first eighth note, the number o on the fifth course corrected to o on the fourth course. Bar 9, third beat, the number 4 on the second course corrected to 3.

Sarabanda: Bar 5, third beat, the number 6 on the second course corrected to 7.

Rhythmic corrections throughout are indicated by square brackets. First and second endings, fermatas, and accent marks are all editorial.

Capriccio-Sarabanda-Capriccio

Francesco Asioli

Concerti armonici per la chitarra spagnuola (Bologna, 1676), 44–48

3. Capriccio

JACARAS—FRANCISCO GUERAU (1694)

Guerau (1649–1722) began his career as a boy soprano in the Royal Chapel in Madrid ca. 1659. He later served as a chamber musician and in 1693 was appointed *Maestro de capilla* at the chapel's school for boy singers. His guitar book, *Poema Harmónico,* was published a year later and is dedicated to Carlos II, the last of the Spanish Habsburg monarchs. Prior to its appearance, hardly any music for baroque guitar had been published in Spain: Juan Carlos y Amat's booklet of 1596, *Guitarra española de cinco ordenes . . .* (earliest surviving edition dated 1626), which contains only a brief example of a piece in Spanish chord notation; Gaspar Sanz's *Instruccion de musica sobre la guitarra española* (1674–75, discussed above); and Lucas Ruiz de Ribayaz's *Luz y norte musical . . .* (1676), in which the music for guitar consists mainly of music by Sanz that has been plagiarized and simplified by Ribayaz.

Guerau's book comprises twenty-seven pieces composed as sets of variations. His compositional style is characterized by its conservatism and nationalistic choice of musical forms. He employs none of the unique idioms that distinguished the guitar from other plucked instruments in Italy and France. Instead, he treats it like a lute, or more fittingly, its counterpart in Spain, the sixteenth- and early seventeenth-century *vihuela.* The music is written almost entirely in *pizzicato* (Spanish: *punteado*) style. Although he doesn't specify stringing, it is clear from the music that he intended bourdons (Spanish: *bordóns*) on both the fourth and fifth courses. In stark contrast to his countrymen Gaspar Sanz and, later, Santiago de Murcia, who adopted the Italian and French composing styles, Guerau seems to have been making a political statement in his style of composing. Ironically, his music, which in its own day was so *un*-guitar-like, is ideal for playing on today's classical guitar.

Originally the *jacaras* was a type of poetry, generally involving rowdy, reprobate characters, which was sung to an improvised melody over a harmonic pattern. In Guerau's time it was a boisterous dance, often performed in stage productions. His version is somewhat typical of the genre in that he uses a harmonic pattern or ground based on two bars of i (D minor) and two bars of V (A major). However, with his occasionally complicated two-part writing and challenging technical demands, it seems more courtly than theatrical and rather serious and passacaglia-like in its effect.

To make the part writing clear, a *tenuto* playing style should be maintained throughout. (For an interpretation of the part writing, refer to the transcription in staff notation below.) After a statement of the basic harmonic pattern in bars 1–8, there follows a long series of variations. I suggest a starting tempo of quarter note = 108. Until bar 45, much of the material is presented in two-part writing. Then the style changes to four bars of slower-moving chromatic chords, followed by a four-bar answer in a different chord voicing. Continuing with a rhythm of running eighth notes, the music seems to want to build in intensity to the downbeat of bar 79, a dramatic and unexpected discord, which can be emphasized with a short fermata. Thereafter, a new style (with a slower, non-regular tempo, perhaps) begins with the series of punctuating slur patterns that grow calmer as they approach bar 85.

After the double bar, it makes sense to return to the original tempo for the bars of two-part writing and to maintain that tempo even when the style changes to strong quarter-note movement in bars 97–104. At bar 104 there's a rapid slur pattern until the calming into eighth notes at bar 111. If the fairly rapid tempo is maintained until the downbeat of bar 119, a powerful, dramatic effect can be achieved—and enhanced if the tempo becomes irregular at the occurrence of the rapid slurs following the down beat. From bar 123, resume the original tempo through the section of dotted rhythms, quarter-note movement, and, at bar 149, an almost arpeggiated two-voice movement, to the stark final octave.

Guerau has two ornament signs in the piece: ✗ (*trino* or *aleado*), which he describes in his preface as a main note trill, and ⟩, which he calls a *mordente*. However, in his description of how the *mordente* is to be played, it is clear that he means not an Italian *mordente* but an ascending appoggiatura. Most other writers use this sign to mean a lower mordent.

A facsimile edition of Guerau's *Poema Harmónico* . . . (Madrid, 1694), published by Tecla (London, 1977) is available from OMI. Another, with an excellent study and transcription for classical guitar, is Thomas Schmitt's *Francisco Guerau: Poema Harmónico*.

Editorial

There are no misprints in the original. The double bars are original, including the irregular one at bar 130. I have left that one as is, since I think it was meant simply to mark the beginning of the new dotted style at that point. I have added accent marks where a *hemiola* pattern is evident. The final bar is editorial.

Jacaras

Francisco Guerau

Poema Harmónico (Madrid, 1694), 35–37

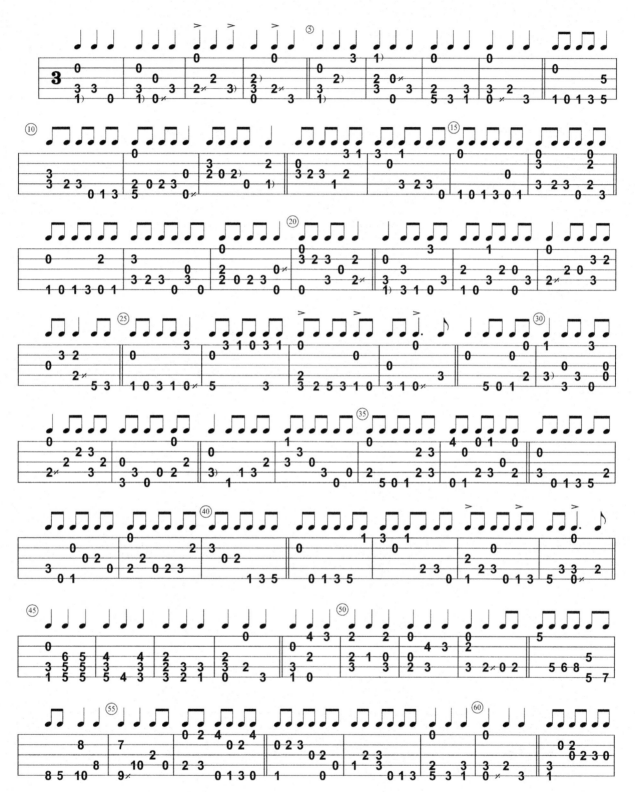

111

Jacaras (continued)

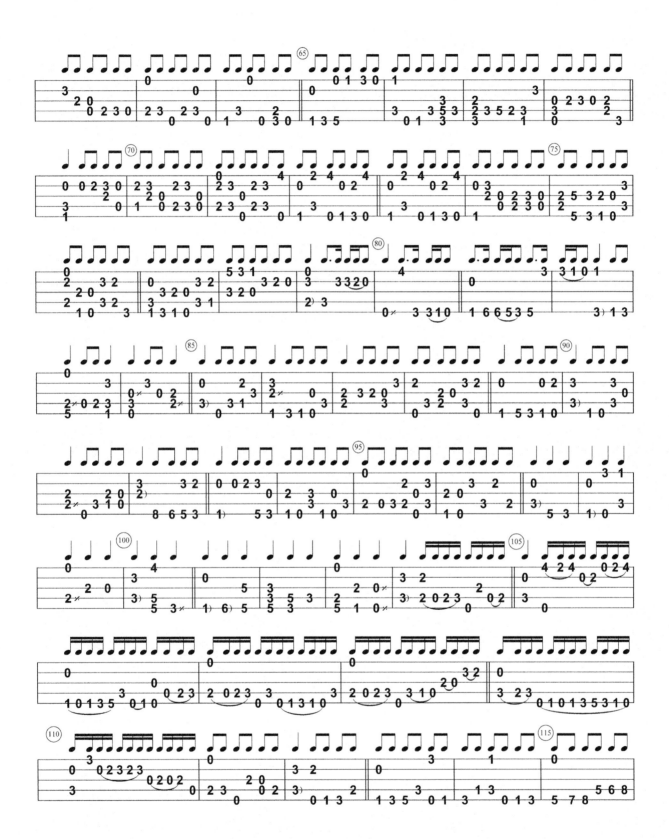

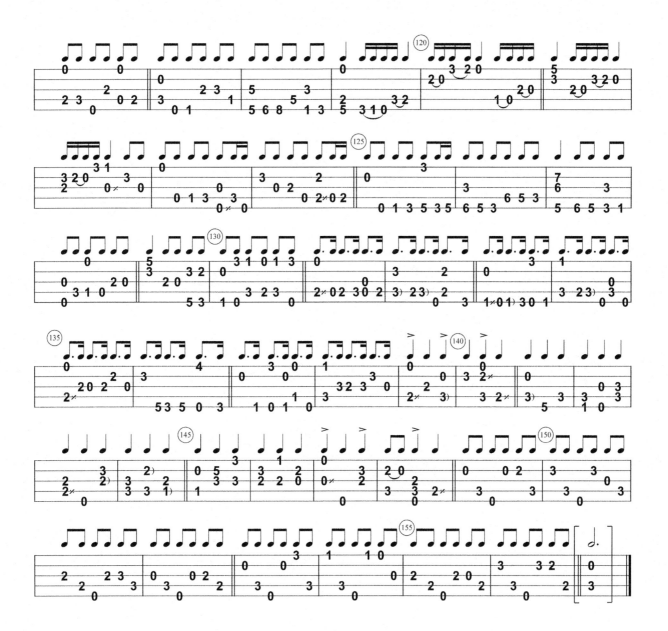

Francisco Guerau, *Jacaras*

Jacaras

115

12

PIECES WITH *BASSO CONTINUO*

SINFONIA A 2—FRANCESCO CORBETTA (1643)

Biographical information about Corbetta can be found in ch. 10 in the commentary that precedes his *Preludio* and *Chiacona*. The terms *sinfonia* and sonata were used interchangeably in the seventeenth century to mean a free-form instrumental piece. Corbetta's *Sinfonia a 2* is from an earlier collection entitled, *Varii capricci per la ghittara spagnuola . . .* (Various Caprices for the Spanish Guitar), published in Milan in 1643. The "*a 2*" indicates that the piece is for a solo instrument (the guitar) and a continuo instrument, such as a lute, theorbo, harpsichord, organ, harp, and so on. In the index to his collection, Corbetta mentions organ or another "basso" (continuo) instrument (*acompagnata con l'organo ò altro Basso*). Indeed, a small chamber organ with wooden pipes and simple eight-foot stops would be an excellent choice. Its muted, transparent, and unobtrusive sound would not overwhelm the guitar's delicate voice. But any of the other named instruments would work equally well if the same level of sensitivity were observed. A bowed instrument to reinforce the bass line is unnecessary and was not expected in Corbetta's time.

For performance, I suggest a fairly slow, dreamy tempo without a steady pulse through bar 12. For the next section, in which the two instruments engage in a lively dialogue, I suggest a steady allegro tempo of half note = 52. The connecting interlude of five bars that follows should be played freely; however, at bar 32, a return to the previous allegro tempo would emphasize the section's more rapid note values and musical activity. At bar 40, or immediately before, I suggest pulling the tempo back in a *rallentando* in preparation for the next section in triple meter. Here, Corbetta employs a device frequently used by his contemporaries, which follows a centuries-old tradition. It seems that players from earlier periods found it easier to read big-value white notes for fast triple time than a staff filled with a long string of smaller value black notes. Some might find this notation a bit confusing, but it actually makes a great deal of sense if one considers that—in those days—the beaming of notes into rhythmic groupings was rare in staff notation and sometimes there weren't even any bar lines!

To add to the confusion, the circle with a line through it in the tablature indicates that the note values are written as double the value of those which came before; that is, instead of the expected three half notes to a bar there are now three whole notes. Fol-

118

lowing the circle is the sign ³₂, which indicates the relationship or proportion of the new three-note units to the previous two-note units in duple time. This proportion was called (in Latin) *sesquialtera*. In this instance, it means that now in triple time, the three-beat units in the bar are to be played in the exact same length of time as the previous two units in duple time. The beat units, in this case, are the two half notes, which correspond to the *tactus*. Normally, when bars change to triple time, they would be comprised of three half notes. But, as will be recalled from the discussion of the *Tactus* system found in ch. 9 in the commentary that precedes Sanz's *Pavanas,* because the *tactus* (the down and up hand motion) doesn't change, the result would be the same as playing a triplet over the previous two beats; that is, the length or speed of the bars remains the same. In the transcription into staff notation (see below), I have given the meter as ³₁, which should help to clarify what's happening in the tablature. The whole notes with double lines on each side are *breves* and are equal to the value of two whole notes.

In this piece, if the duple time allegros are half note = 53, then (assuming my algebra is correct), the triple time whole notes should each be 78. The sections from bar 41 to 60, therefore, should be regarded as quite dance-like. The final three bars are a little reprise of the previous three, and, given Corbetta's own *piano* marking, I suggest playing them slower as well as gentler for a nicely subtle conclusion to the piece.

Only one ornament sign is present in the original tablature, .T., which I interpret to mean a main note trill, as would be expected for Italian music of this period.

A facsimile edition of Corbetta's *Varii capricci per la ghittara spagnuola . . .* (Milan, 1643), published by Archivium Musicum (Florence, 1980), is available from OMI.

Editorial

There are only a few misprints in the original. Bar 10, guitar: the first two notes are given as eighths, but have been corrected to sixteenths. Bar 15, basso: a sharp appears next to the quarter note d, but is actually a continuo figure. Bar 23, basso: a flat appears next to the note d, but is actually a continuo figure 6. Bar 38, basso: the note b has been corrected to b flat.

I believe this piece is suitable for stringing B and have transcribed it as such. Editorial additions are double bar lines to mark sections, except the one at bar 26, which is original; accent marks in the triple meter sections to indicate *hemiolas,* as made clear in the basso part; asterisks below the tablature to indicate the inclusion of the fourth-course bourdon, and dots on the staves to indicate selective chord voicing. Corbetta's original *piano* marking has been moved from bar 62 to 61. In the basso part, continuo figures above the staff are those found in the original; those below the staff are editorial.

Sinfonia a 2

Francesco Corbetta

Varii capricci per la ghitarra spagnuola (Milan, 1643), 77–81

120

Sinfonia a 2 (continued)

122

Sinfonia a 2 (continued)

SINFONIA À DUI—GIOVANNI BATTISTA GRANATA (1651)

Granata's biographical details can be found in ch. 10 in the commentary that precedes his suite of pieces from 1674. The present work is from an interesting earlier collection entitled, *Nuova Scielta di capricci armonici* (New Selection of Harmonic Caprices) published in Bologna in 1651. It is, of course, in the same genre as Corbetta's *Sinfonia a 2;* that is, a sonata for solo guitar with continuo accompaniment.

The first eight bars of the piece can be regarded as a prelude and played somewhat slowly and without a steady tempo. At the start of the eighth-note scale at bar 9 in the basso line, establish a steady, cheerful allegro tempo of half note = 62. From bars 9–23 there's a playful dialogue between the two instruments with a brief passage of parallel sixths in bars 13 and 14. The triple time section at bar 24 should also remain brisk at about quarter note = 114. The piece is a well-wrought example of (basically) two-part contrapuntal writing for the guitar, and therefore should be played with as much left-hand *tenuto* technique as possible, despite the technical difficulties that maintaining this style might present. In preparation for the next change of style and texture, a slowdown is recommended just before the new duple time section begins at bar 39.

At the change of meter, it is the basso that sets the tempo, perhaps half note = 62. This section is written in a two-part fugal style and should remain at a steady tempo, building in intensity until it reaches the climactic bar, 57. Treat the middle of bar 57 through bar 59 like a *dénouement* cadence point—slowing down and relaxing; and play bar 60 to the conclusion slowly and in a free tempo, dwelling on many of the eighth notes (such as the ones in bar 62), to suggest a contemplative postlude to the piece.

The ornament signs in the tablature consist of: *t:* for a main note trill and *.t.* for an ornament of the player's choice. At some points, such as in bar 22, parallel trills are marked. The signs at bars 50 and 59 in the original tablature were tiny, poorly printed, and hard to read. They look like *.#.*, but are probably misprinted trill marks. If not, they could possibly indicate a lower mordent. Granata does not explain his ornament signs.

The letter H7 chord with a small cross next to it on the second course in bar 22 means that it should be played as a discord by placing the fourth finger of the left hand at fret 10, thus producing a 5/4 chord on E, which resolves to a 5/3 chord in the remainder of the bar.

A facsimile edition of Granata's *Nuova Scielta di capricci armonici* . . . (Bologna, 1651), published by Forni (Bologna, 1991), is available from OMI.

Editorial

The following corrections have been made to the original tablature. Bar 5, guitar: the first note of the rhythm is printed as a white eighth note, corrected to a regular dotted eighth note. Bar 7, guitar: the fourth sixteenth note, given as number 8, corrected to 9. Bar 9 guitar: rhythm printed as two tied half notes, corrected to a whole note. Bar 12, guitar: rhythm printed as quarter note tied to a dotted half note, corrected to a whole note. Bar 16, guitar: rhythm printed as two tied half notes, corrected to a whole note. Bar 21, basso: first note given as f natural, corrected to f sharp. Bar 22, guitar: last eighth note printed as quarter note. Bars 39 and 46, guitar: rhythm printed as two tied half notes, corrected to whole notes. Bar 63, guitar: the printed tie from the half note rest to the first sixteenth note is redundant and I have eliminated it.

I believe this piece is suitable for stringing B, and I have transcribed it as such. The bar lines are irregular in the original, and I have made them consistent. Double bar lines are editorial except those at bars 23 and 38, which are original. Granata's tablature number x has been changed to 10, and ij to 11. My asterisks below the tablature staff have been added to indicate that the lower bourdon should be included on the fourth course at those points.

Sinfonia à dui

Giovanni Battista Granata

Nuova Scielta di capriccio armonici (Bologna, 1651), Book III, 53–59

Sinfonia à dui (continued)

130

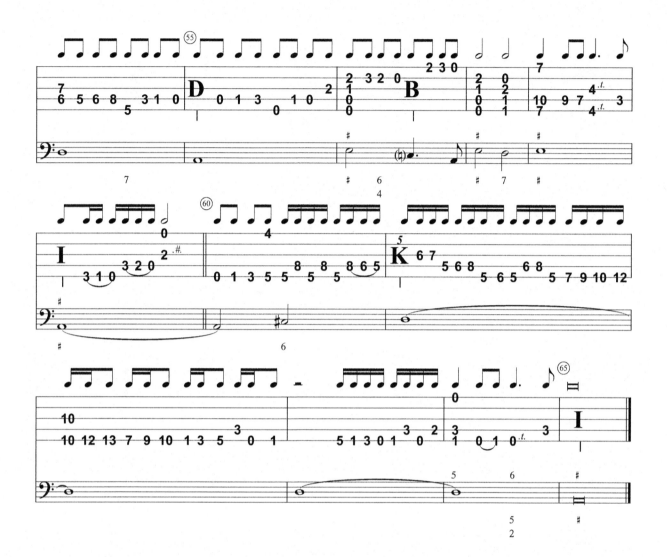

131

Giovanni Battista Granata, *Sinfonia à dui*

133

Sinfonia à dui (continued)

FOLLIÀ: SONATA 12 DE CORELI [SIC] —ARCANGELO CORELLI/ANONYMOUS (CA. 1725–30)

This is a setting, or arrangement, of a sonata for violin and *basso continuo* by the renowned violinist and composer of string sonatas and concertos Arcangelo Corelli (1653–1713). It is included in an anonymous manuscript of guitar and violin music now housed in the National Library in Mexico City (MS 1560), and dates from between 1725 and 1730. It's possible that it was brought to Mexico from Spain at around that time. The compiler copied several items into the manuscript from the guitar books of Gaspar Sanz (1674) and Santiago de Murcia (1714), as well as guitar arrangements of sonatas from Corelli's famous opus 5 collection of sonatas published in Rome in 1700. The arrangements are presumed to be the compiler's own and do not include the bass lines.

The present sonata is a set of variations on the well known *folia* harmonic pattern, which is discussed in ch. 10 in the commentary that precedes François Le Cocq's *Folies d'Espagne*. The guitar part, mostly sounding an octave lower, is by and large a quite skillful arrangement of the violin part. Because it does not appear in the manuscript, I have added Corelli's original basso part from the 1700 print. The anonymous arranger has used only twelve of Corelli's twenty-three variations. For reference, the correspondence between the manuscript and printed variations are: manuscript variations 1–5 = Corelli 1–5 (except the guitar part for 2 is the arranger's own); manuscript variation 6 = Corelli 7; manuscript variation 7 = Corelli 9; manuscript variation 8 = Corelli 10; manuscript variation 9 = Corelli 11; manuscript variation 10 = Corelli 12; manuscript variation 11 = Corelli 13; and manuscript variation 12 = Corelli 14. The guitar part is reasonably faithful to the violin part, but many octave displacements and other remedies have been used to adapt the music to the guitar's range capabilities and idioms.

The opening statement of the harmonic pattern is very difficult if one plays all the ornaments called for in the tablature. To do so requires the careful planning of alternative left-hand fingerings. Original tempo indications for several of the variations are given, which makes interpreting them somewhat easier and metronome markings unnecessary. As always, *tenuto* technique (with the left-hand fingers remaining on chords or individual notes until it is absolutely necessary to let go) should be employed, and the original diagonal lines in variation 6 point to this style of playing. Much use is made of arpeggios and there are many passages of *campanelas*. In some of the variations—number 8 for example—the solo and continuo instruments engage in animated dialogue.

A word should be said about the first eight bars of variation 7. Frankly, it is difficult to make any sense of them in the anonymous arranger's tablature. It appears as if he attempted to depart from Corelli's original violin part and, having made a mess of it, gave up after the first eight bars and went back to the original violin part for the remainder of the section! In my edition, I have substituted an intabulation of Corelli's *original* first eight bars, and I have also reproduced the anonymous arranger's first eight bars in an appendix that can be found at the conclusion of the tablature version of the piece. Apart from some minor flaws, however, the arranger has created an exciting and idiomatic guitar sonata from one of Corelli's most famous violin sonatas.

The ornament signs appear to follow those of Santiago de Murcia. In bars 4 and 12, ✗ with a tiny auxiliary number near it signifies a main note trill and the fret number to hammer up to. Bar 145 has parallel trill signs, but the lower one seems to be a misprint because when holding down the chord, there's only one spare finger left for the ornament. The comma sign indicates a descending appoggiatura.

There is no facsimile edition of the manuscript that contains this guitar sonata; however, a facsimile of Corelli's op. 5, published by Archivium Musicum (Florence, 1979), is available from OMI.

Editorial

There are a number of errors in the original tablature. Bar 38: the second eighth note given as number 6, corrected to 5. Bar 57: the fifth eighth note given as number 6, corrected to 7. Bar 83: the eighth sixteenth note given as 0 on the fourth course, corrected to 6 on the second course. Bar 87: the sixth sixteenth note given as number 5, corrected to 6. Bar 110: the fourth sixteenth note given as 0, corrected to 2. Bar 121: there is a $\frac{3}{8}$ meter sign at the beginning of the bar, which is clearly meant for the next section. Bar 126: the N3 *alfabeto* chord given is corrected to P.3 Bars 146 and 150: in the half-note chord the numbers on the fourth course given as 3 are corrected to 5. Bars 156 and 157: the last eighth notes given as number 5 are corrected to 6.

I believe this piece is suitable for stringing B, and I have transcribed it as such. For the continuo part, I've used Corelli's bass line but have applied my own figures. Square brackets are used in the tablature to indicate other minor corrections, and I have added accent marks to indicate *hemiolas*. My asterisks below the staff indicate that a bourdon on the fourth course should be included at those points, and dots on staff lines have been added to indicate selective chord voicing.

Follià: Sonata 12 de Coreli [*sic*]

Arcangelo Corelli/
Anonymous

Mexico City, Biblioteca Nacional, MS 1560, fols. 33v–36v (ca. 1725–30)

Follià: Sonata 12 de Coreli (continued)

Follià: Sonata 12 de Coreli

139

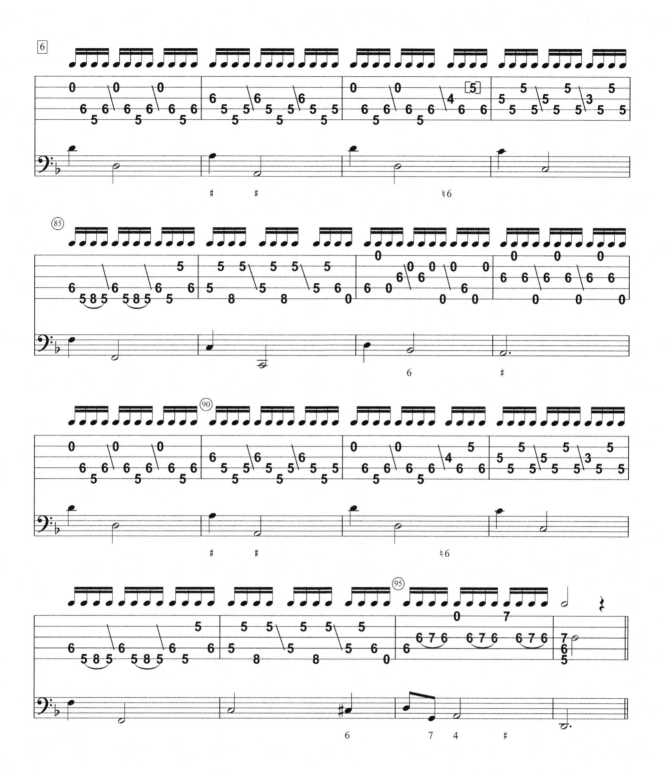

Follià: Sonata 12 de Coreli (continued)

144

Follià: Sonata 12 de Coreli

Appendix

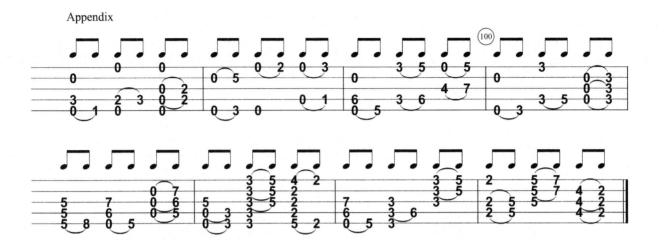

146

Follià: Sonata 12 de Coreli

Follià: Sonata 12 de Coreli (continued)

150

Follià: Sonata 12 de Coreli

153

SELECTED BIBLIOGRAPHY

Ashworth, Jack, and Paul O'Dette. "Basso Continuo." In *A Performer's Guide to Seventeenth-Century Music.* New York: Schirmer Books, 1997, 269–89.

Boye, Gary R. *Giovanni Battista Granata and the Development of Printed Music for the Guitar in Seventeenth-Century Italy.* Ph.D. diss., Duke University, 1995.

Brown, Elizabeth C. D. "Early Guitar Technique: A Little Advice." *Lute Society Quarterly* 41/3 (2006): 4–9.

Hall, Monica. "The Five-Course Guitar as a Continuo Instrument." *Lute News: The Lute Society Magazine,* no. 52 (December 1999): 11–15.

Koonce, Frank. *The Baroque Guitar in Spain and the New World: Gaspar Sanz, Antonio de Santa Cruz, Francisco Guerau, Santiago de Murcia.* Pacific, Mo.: Mel Bay Publications, 2006. (This is an excellent discussion and anthology of music of the Spanish composers named. The transcriptions are made specifically for classical guitar.)

North, Nigel. *Continuo Playing on the Lute, Archlute and Theorbo.* Bloomington: Indiana University Press, 1987.

Russell, Craig H. "François Le Cocq: Belgian Master of the Baroque Guitar." *Soundboard* 15/4 (Winter 1988–89): 288–93.

Schmitt, Thomas. *Francisco Guerau: Poema Harmónico compuerto de varias cifras per al temple de la guitarra española.* Madrid: Editorial Alpuerto, 2000.

Sor, Fernando. *Method for the Spanish Guitar by Ferdinand Sor.* Trans. A. Merrick. [ca. 1850]. New York: Da Capo Press, 1980.

Treadwell, Nina. "Guitar Alfabeto in Italian Monody: The Publications of Alessandro Vincenti." *The Lute,* no. 33 (1993): 12–22.

Tyler, James. Introduction to the facsimile edition of: *G. B. Granata: Soavi Concenti di Sonate (1659).* Monaco: Éditions Chanterelle, 1979.

———. Introduction to the facsimile edition of: *Nicola Matteis: The False Consonances of Musick (1682).* Monaco: Éditions Chanterelle, 1980.

———. "The Role of the Guitar in the Rise of Monody: The Earliest Manuscripts." *Journal of Seventeenth-Century Music* 9/1 (2004). Available at www.jscm.org/jsm/v9/no1/Tyler.html.

Tyler, James, and Paul Sparks. *The Guitar and Its Music from the Renaissance to the Classical Era.* Oxford/New York: Oxford University Press, 2007. (Contains a survey of the entire repertoire, detailed information on signs, ornaments, etc., and tables listing almost every known source of early guitar music. It also lists the sources available in facsimile editions.)

WEBSITES

The Baroque Guitar: Printed Music from 1606–1737 (Gary R. Boye)
  http://www.library.appstate.edu/music/guitar/home.html
  Gives details and contents of every known Italian printed source.

Early Guitars and Vihuela
  http://earlyguitar.ning.com
  A social networking site that sometimes contains useful information.

The Lute Society (of Great Britain)
  http://www.lutesoc.co.uk

Journal of Seventeenth-Century Music
  http://www.jscm.org.html

Monica Hall: Baroque Guitar Research
  http://www.monicahall.co.uk
  Contains music articles on Corbetta, Foscarini, Bartolotti, Le Cocq, and others.

OMI (Old Manuscripts & Incunabula)
  http://www.omnifacsimiles.com/
  An internet bookseller. Carries virtually all known facsimile editions of early guitar music.

Rebours, Gérard
  http://g.rebours.free.fr/Articles-GerardRebours.htm
  Contains useful articles and information on French guitarists.

INDEX

Page numbers in italics indicate musical examples.

charango, 25

chiacona. See ciaccona

Chigi, Cardinal Flavio, 65

chitarriglia, 101

cheute. See appoggiatura

chitarra spagnola, 3, 101

Christina, Queen of Sweden, 70

ciaccona, 50, 65. *See also* grounds

ciacona. See ciaccona

cifras, 10

classical guitar, vii–viii, 3–4, 6–7, 10, 13, 32, 97, 109

Le Cocq, François, 80–81; *Folies d'Espagne,* 80–81, *82–95*

Colista, Lelio, 12, 33, 65–66; *Passacaille dite Mariona,* 12, 65–66, *67–69. See also* Castillon, Jean Baptiste de

Collegio de Nobili di Parma, 105

Colonna, Giovanni Antonio, 28; *Balletto* [Almande Prince, Pavan of Albart, *Si je m'en vois*], *28–29*

Concerto Palatino, 57

coranto. See corrente

Corbetta, Francesco, 45, 49–51, 70, 101, 118–119; *Chiacona,* 50–51, *53–55; Prelud[io],* 49–51, *52, 55; Sinfonia a 2,* 118–119, *120–125,* 126; *Varii capricci per la ghittara spagnuola,* 118–119; *Varii scherzo di sonate per la chitarra spagnola,* 49, 51–53

Corelli, Arcangelo, 65, 135–136; and Anonymous: *Follià: Sonata 12 de Coreli* [*sic*], 135–136, *137–153;* in Mexico City, Biblioteca Nacional, MS 1560, 135; *Sonate, op. 5,* 135–136

Corgna, Fabio della, 97

corrente, 41, 57

Corrette, Michel, 25

courante. See corrente

course(s), 3–4, *5. See also* tuning and stringing

Cromwell, Elizabeth, 37

diagonal mark (line), *17,* 18, 66

Don Juan of Austria, 33

Elizabeth, Electress Palatine and Queen of Bohemia, 45

esmorsata. See appoggiatura

Este, Francesco II d', Duke of Modena and Reggio, 105

Ferdinand Karl, Archduke of Innsbruck, 70

figured bass. *See basso continuo*

flamenco, 13

folia, 80, 135. *See also* grounds

folies. See folia

follià. See folia

Foscarini, Giovanni Paolo, 14, 18, 22, 96–97; *alfabeto dissonante,* 22; *Li cinque libri della chitarra alla spagnola,* 97; *Pavaniglia con parti variate,* 96–97, *98–100; Il primo, second, e terzo libro della chitarra spagnola,* 96–97

Frederick V, Elector Palatine and King of Bohemia, 45

French tablature, 11–12, *11, 12*

frets, 3, 8

Furioso, Il. *See* Foscarini, Giovanni Paolo

galant, 76

giga, 57

graces. *See* ornaments

Granata, Giovanni Battista, 57–58, 126–127; *Alemanda,* 57–58, *59, 63; Corrente,* 57–58, *60, 63; Giga,* 57–58, *62, 64; Sarabanda,* 57–58, *61, 64; Novi capricci armonici musicali,* 57, 59; *Nuova Scielta di capricci armonici;* 126; *Sinfonia à dui,* 126–127, *128–134*

grounds, 109. *See also* Anonymous (*Aria di Fiorenza*); Bergamasca; *ciaccona; folia; mariona; passacaglia*

Guerau, Francisco, 109–110; *Jacaras,* 109–110, *111–117; Poema Harmónico,* 109–110

habilidades. See ornaments

Hall, Monica: "The Five-Course Guitar as a Continuo Instrument," 28

hemiola, 50–51, 66, 81, 105, 110, 119, 136

Hindemith, Paul, ix

"I Know Not What/a Gigge [Jig]," 37, *39–40*

Iadone, Joseph, ix

"inversionless" chords, 23

Italian monody, 23

Italian tablature, 8–11, *9–11*

stracini. See slurs
Stradivari, Antonio, 25
stroke signs, 12, 81
strum. *See battuto;* simple strokes

tablature, vii, 8–12. *See also alfabeto;* French
    tablature; Italian tablature; mixed
    tablature
Tactus system, 34, 119
Talbot, James, 45
technique, 6–7. *See also battuto;* left-hand
    position; nails; rhythmic ornamentation;
    right-hand technique; simple strokes
temblor. See vibrato
tenuto, 16–17, 50, 70, 76, 97, 109, 126, 135
tiple, 25
Treadwell, Nina, x
tremblement. See trill, upper-note
tremoli. See ornaments
tremolo. See trill
tremolo sforzato. See vibrato
trill, 19–20; main note trills, 19, 33, 37, 49, 57,
    65, 97, 105, 110, 119, 126, 136; upper note
    trills, 20, 45, 49, 65, 76

trillo, 14, *15*
trino. See trill
tuning and stringing, 3–4, *5*, 12, 25, 33, 37,
    41, 45, 50, 109, 119. *See also* re-entrant,
    scordatura

universal *alfabeto* reference chart, *21*

Valdembrini, Ferdinando, 41; *Corrente nona,*
    41, *42–44; Libro primo d'intavolatura di*
    chitarra, 42
vertical mark (line), *17*, 18, 65, 76
vibrato, 18, 33, 50, 57, 97, 105
vihuela, 109

William III of the Netherlands and King of
    England, 45

zarabanda. See sarabanda
Ziani, Pietro Andrea, 33

JAMES TYLER

studied lute with Joseph Iadone and early music performance with Thomas Binkley. He spent his early career performing and recording with such ensembles as the New York Pro Musica, Musica Reservata, the Consort of Musicke, and the Early Music Consort of London under David Munrow. He joined the Julian Bream Consort in 1975 and a year later founded the London Early Music Group. With these ensembles, he performed in chamber music series and festivals throughout Europe, North America, Asia, the Middle East, and Australia, made more than sixty recordings, and appeared on TV and in films. He is a featured soloist on recordings with the English Concert, the Academy of St. Martin in the Fields, and Max Morath's Original Rag Quartet. He served as Professor of Music History and Literature, Director of the Early Music Program, and Director of the Thornton Baroque Sinfonia at the University of Southern California until his retirement in 2006. He is author of *The Early Guitar: A History and Handbook* and, with Paul Sparks, of *The Guitar and Its Music* and *The Early Mandolin*.

CPSIA information can be obtained
at www.ICGtesting.com
Printed in the USA
BVOW09s1108151216

470888BV00017B/49/P